Internal Migration During Modernization in Late Nineteenth-Century Russia

INTERNAL MIGRATION DURING MODERNIZATION IN LATE NINETEENTH-CENTURY RUSSIA

Barbara A. Anderson

PRINCETON UNIVERSITY PRESS
PRINCETON, NEW JERSEY

Publication of this book has been aided by the Whitney
Darrow Publication Reserve Fund of Princeton University Press

This book has been composed in VIP Times Roman

Clothbound editions of Princeton University Press books
are printed on acid-free paper, and binding materials are
chosen for strength and durability

Printed in the United States of America by Princeton
University Press, Princeton, New Jersey

To my husband

CONTENTS

LIST OF TABLES

LIST OF FIGURES

LIST OF MAPS

PREFACE

Over the past twenty years, an increasing amount of attention has been focused on problems of internal migration and related problems of overcrowding of cities in currently developing countries. However, these issues are very difficult to study in currently developing countries because the data collection systems in such countries are often not well-developed and because the outcomes of current patterns will not be known until the future.

The difficulties of studying internal migration in currently developing countries and especially in testing the model of migration that I propose led me to study internal migration in a major historical case, Russia. Japan and Russia are the prime examples of successful latecomers to modernization. I argue that an understanding of internal migration in Russia in the late nineteenth century is relevant to the understanding of internal migration in currently developing countries. By the late nineteenth century, the Russian Empire had a well-developed statistical system, and the 1897 census allows me to study in detail many issues that would be more problematic to study in many currently developing countries. Also, we know that Russia became one of the most highly developed societies in the twentieth century.

Because this is a work of social science that tests an explicit model of internal migration during modernization on a particular case, Russia in the late nineteenth century, it is not primarily a work about Russian history. Particular facts concerning Russian history are included only to the extent necessary to demonstrate that the arguments presented are reasonable and to acquaint the reader with enough Russian history to understand what is presented.

Although the primary contribution of this work is in the understanding of migration during modernization, some new facts about Russian history are also revealed. For instance, the pattern of migration to Asiatic Russia is analyzed somewhat differently from earlier work on the subject and the stability of the pattern of migration to Moscow and St. Petersburg cities throughout the last half of the nineteenth century is documented. Hopefully, both the general and the specific findings will be of some interest to historians, as well as to sociologists, economists, demographers, and geographers.

This work is a revised version of a dissertation that I wrote at Princeton University in 1974. Many people contributed both to that dissertation and to the revisions that I have made since then. Ansley Coale introduced me to demography, while Marion Levy, Jr., Allen Kassof, Cyril Black, Gilbert Rozman, and Frederick Shorter helped me to understand the concepts and literature in comparative studies and modernization. Cyril Black and S. Frederick Starr taught me about nineteenth-century Russian society.

These various interests came together in the dissertation topic suggested by S. Frederick Starr in Spring 1971. Charles Wheatley was exceedingly helpful in turning vague ideas into explicit interconnected hypotheses. William Seltzer, Donald Heisel, and Thomas Burch were also helpful in clarifying many of my thoughts about internal migration. If this work is readable and understandable to persons from a variety of disciplines, a large part of the credit goes to Cyril Black, who always encouraged clarity and comprehensibility. Frederick Shorter, Ansley Coale, and Jane Menken were helpful on many technical and statistical questions. Beth Kaplowitz, D. Eleanor Westney, Jonathan Hamilton, Michael Haines, Brian Silver, Susan Tiano, Calvin

Goldscheider, Patricia Herlihy, Richard Crecco, Victoria King, and Frederick Skinner have also read and offered helpful comments on various parts. Although he was not directly involved in this research, I must also thank Melvin Tumin for general intellectual guidance and support over the years. I am grateful to Academic Press and to the Center for Advanced Study in the Behavioral Sciences for permission to use some material that appeared in my chapter, "Who Chose the Cities?: Migrants to Moscow and St. Petersburg Cities in the Late Nineteenth Century," in R. Lee, ed., *Population Patterns in the Past*, Academic Press, New York 1977, copyright held by Center for Advanced Study in the Behavioral Sciences.

The original dissertation research was supported by a National Institutes of Health Traineeship in Demography and part of the thesis preparation was supported by a grant from the National Science Foundation, NSF GS-31730X2, at the Institute for Advanced Study. The preparation of the book manuscript was aided by grants from the Darrow Fund of Princeton University Press and the Faculty Development Fund at Brown University. Expert typing was supplied by Joyce Coleman and Norma MacDonald.

*Internal Migration During Modernization
in Late Nineteenth-Century Russia*

CHAPTER 1

Introduction

THE PROBLEM

Many researchers have contended that internal migration during a country's period of industrialization is primarily a response to better opportunities at the destination when these opportunities are compared to those at the origin of migration. This study contends that a person's attitudes may be just as important and often are more important in determining his migration status and choice of destination. In a society where modern attitudes such as willingness to work in industry and to move to unfamiliar places are not distributed uniformly, persons with more modern attitudes may be more willing to migrate than others, even though persons with less modern attitudes might experience a greater increase in expected income or standard of living through migration. This study concentrates on those characteristics of man's geographical origins that shape both the environment which influences the potential migrant's decision whether to migrate and his choice of destination.

The proposed model considers two basic types of migration during modernization. These types are differentiated by the nature of the destination. The first type is migration to a destination in an already settled, relatively modern area. This kind of migration, associated with industrialization and urbanization, often responds to urban industrial opportunities. The second type is migration to a destination in a frontier area where the land was previously sparsely populated.

Migration to such a frontier destination is often precipitated by disadvantageous conditions at the origin.

The two types of destinations are expected to be differentially attractive to persons according to their socialization. Migration within a settled area should appeal to persons from environments that would lead them to have relatively modern attitudes. Such places would have a relatively high literacy rate, a high degree of modernization of industry, and a low birth rate. Traditional agriculture would be relatively unimportant. Migrants choosing a destination within a settled area, especially one of the most highly developed destinations, would be moving as much due to a recognition of opportunities elsewhere and a positive attitude toward risk taking involved in migration as to the objective chance of economic gain brought about by migration.

Migration to a frontier, on the other hand, should appeal to persons who want to pursue a traditional agricultural type of life in a setting similar to that at their origin but in a location where land and personal freedom would be more readily available. Such persons would not be eager to accept all aspects of modern life. Their move would be motivated by population pressure at their origin to a greater extent than would be the case for migrants within a settled area. Migrants choosing a frontier destination would generally come from places with a relatively low literacy rate and a low degree of modernization of industry, where traditional agriculture was virtually the only means of support.

This research tests the model for persons born in European Russia who lived in the Russian Empire in the last half of the nineteenth century. European Russia at that time was a modernizing society, with rapidly growing industry and increasing literacy. Thus this area is an appropriate setting in which to test this model. Migration to either Moscow City or St. Petersburg City provides the major example of migration to a settled modern destination; migration to Asiatic Russia exemplifies migration to an agricultural frontier. Destinations of intermediate modernity between the two great cities and Asiatic Russia are also considered in order to determine the model's accuracy.

THEORETICAL BASIS

This study of social change in modernization requires clarification of the term modernization. Cyril Black defines modernization as "the process by which historically evolved institutions are adapted to the rapidly changing functions that reflect the unprecedented increase in man's knowledge, permitting control over his environment, that accompanied the scientific revolution" (Black 1966: 7). More concisely, it is "a process by which the traditional institutions are adapted to modern functions" (Black 1966: 46). Black's definition stresses the importance of knowledge in a period of rapid change and thus emphasizes a cultural aspect of modernization.

Another aspect of modernization involves industrialization. Marion J. Levy, Jr. (1966: 11) uses an industrial criterion to differentiate relatively modernized from relatively non-modernized societies. In Levy's view, the greater the ratio of inanimate to animate power used, the more modernized the society. Animate sources of power are men and animals, while inanimate sources are primarily machines.

E. A. Wrigley divides modernization explicitly into both cultural and industrial components. The cultural aspect includes an increase in literacy, an increase in the proportion of the population living in urban areas, conscious control of marital fertility, and an expanded world view; the industrial aspect includes an increase in per capita gross national product and the utilization of modern production methods

(Wrigley 1969; Bendix 1967: 29). Cultural and industrial modernization usually occur together, although not always in perfect coordination nor in any set order. England was quite industrialized before it experienced a substantial increase in literacy, while the opposite was true for France (Wrigley 1969).

The cultural aspect of modernization is closely related to psychological changes during modernization. In a stable, relatively unchanging society, adherence to traditional ways of doing things is likely to lead to success. Such adherence to established methods is especially typical of agricultural life, where vagaries of weather encourage a conservative mode of operation (Redfield and Rojas 1962). When declining mortality causes population increase but there is little or no technological improvement in agricultural technique, a common response is intensification of agriculture through long-known methods.[1] Clifford Geertz (1963) and Ester Boserup (1970) have pointed out that this was clearly observable in parts of Indonesia. They argue that once intensification occurs, requiring more man-hours of labor per unit of yield, the social structure changes in such a way that it becomes increasingly resistant to modern, innovative change. In this manner, the relative importance of intensive, traditional agriculture among various areas may affect the ability of persons from different areas to respond posi-

[1] Although mortality decline is thought to be the most common cause of increases in population growth rates in early stages of modernization, increases in fertility are also possible and would have the same effect. For a discussion of causes of population growth in early modern Europe, see McKeown (1976). For a discussion of some of the ways in which fertility increases may affect population growth, see Anderson and McCabe (1977). Any decrease in the age of female marriage would also be likely to lead to higher overall fertility and thus high population growth rates. For effects of marriage age on fertility and thus growth rates, see Lesthaeghe (1971).

tively to the kinds of changes that occur during the modernization of their society.

In a premodern society, a person interacts primarily with members of his family and others he has known throughout his life. These premodern interaction patterns differ substantially from those common in a modernizing society. Modernization increases the degree of dependence on and the frequency of interaction with strangers and other persons whom one sees only in a limited range of contexts. This change in the nature of interpersonal contacts requires a major adjustment that may be stressful for the individual (Simmel 1960: 437-448; Levy 1972: 56-59). Regardless of a person's sex or occupation, a willingness to take risks is generally more important in a society in which economic conditions are changing rapidly than in a more stable society (Lewis 1955: 42-44).

Alex Inkeles and David Smith (1974) have amassed impressive evidence for the existence of a modern personality. The modern person is more willing to take risks and to consult with others in making decisions, and he has a broader world view than the less modern man. In their study, they found the more modern person also exhibited fewer psychosomatic symptoms than his less modern counterpart.

Some researchers have questioned whether migrants to major urban areas in developing countries are actually selected from those at the origin for possession of relatively modern characteristics. The presence of kin in urban areas is thought by many to be decisive in the decision to move to a city (Flinn and Converse 1970; Kemper 1971), and many migrant neighborhoods in cities are characterized as transplanted (and relatively unchanged) peasant villages (Abu-Lughod 1971). However, Peter Chi and Mark Bogan (1974) found evidence that both migrants to Lima and those who expressed a desire to migrate in the future differed substantially in possession of modern attitudes from those who expressed no desire ever to migrate to Peru's major city. They conducted a survey of residents of four villages near Lima and of natives of those villages who had already migrated to the city. Each person in the survey was asked whether he would be willing to migrate to a place where he had no friends or relatives. Comparing males, the migrants were more often willing to do this than were those who remained in the villages (66 percent versus 35 percent). When those who remained in the villages were divided according to whether or not they ever wanted to migrate to Lima, of those who wanted to migrate in the indeterminate future, 51 percent expressed a willingness to migrate to a place where they had no friends or relatives, while only 27 percent of those with no desire to migrate expressed such a willingness. Also 68 percent of the non-migrants who wanted to leave (both sexes combined) expressed a willingness for their children to move away in the future, while only 49 percent of those with no desire to leave expressed such a willingness.

This is a study of one pattern of change in modernization—migration within a society, or internal migration. Patterns of migration often change during a society's modernization: new industrial opportunities as well as changing attitudes toward seeking such opportunities often cause an increase in the volume of migration (Gugler 1969; Eisenstadt 1966: 10-11, 20-21), and there is often a change in the pattern of origins and destinations. William Petersen (1958) has offered a conceptualization of the transformation of the nature of migration during modernization as "pioneering" to "mass." According to this conception, the most adventurous persons are the first to migrate, while later, after migration has become more common, migration is less selective of persons with advanced skills or adventuresome attitudes.

There is an ongoing debate concerning whether or under what conditions migrants become more conservative or more adventuresome. Goldstein (1971) found evidence that in Thailand recent migrants to major cities had lower fertility rates than did longer duration migrants to such cities, while for major cities in the Philippines, Hendershot (1971) interpreted his evidence as supporting the opposite pattern. Thus in terms of fertility behavior, Goldstein's evidence suggests that the selection of migrants changes from (somewhat) "mass" to "pioneering," while Hendershot's evidence suggests a development from "pioneering" to "mass."

Many persons who have studied internal migration in currently developing countries have viewed potential migrants as rational men who decide whether to migrate and thus choose a destination after determining (even if subconsciously) which behavior would maximize expected income or effect the greatest increase in one's standard of living (Todaro 1969: 138-148; Harris and Todaro 1970; Jorgenson 1961: 309-334). William Leasure and Robert A. Lewis (1968) assumed that such a mechanism determined migration in their interesting study of migration in Russia.

The expectation that objectively assessed economic gain is the primary cause of migration is related to the common assumption that the major factor motivating migration from rural areas is "population pressure" (Simmons, Diaz-Briquets, and Laquian 1977: 53). Geroid Robinson (1969: 106-111) assumed that migration to industrial centers for wage work in late nineteenth-century European Russia was primarily the result of impoverished peasants being forced off the land by intolerable crowding and increasing poverty. In his generally excellent study of urban growth in nineteenth-century Russia, Thomas Fedor (1975) also subscribes to this view.

Any person may compare his likely fate in his present place of residence and at various possible destinations in order to decide whether to migrate and which destination to choose. However, such a rational calculation is only possible within the limits of the opportunities already known to the person and under the circumstances that the person would consider migration a realistic possibility. Simmons, Diaz-Briquets, and Laquian (1977: 25) point out that, although there is little empirical evidence, most researchers have assumed that even those migrants who actually move to a city often have a very inaccurate view of actual labor market conditions at their destination. If this is the case, it casts doubt on the accuracy with which such individual calculations could be made.

There has been a similar debate about the extent to which economic factors motivate persons to voluntarily control marital fertility. In a study of Haiti, Stycos (1968: 116-132) amassed a great deal of evidence showing that not only was the decision whether to attempt family planning not made as a result of the calculation of relative economic advantage but that the vast majority of the population did not even perceive any relationship between the number of children a family had and the family's economic well-being. Many studies of the adoption of family planning have shown that the first persons to adopt such strategies are usually those who are relatively well-off economically and would not be likely to experience as proportionately great a saving from reducing their fertility as would poorer families (Wrigley 1969: 185-202; Davtyan 1966; Sinha 1957).

Thus, in a society where persons differ greatly in their knowledge of opportunities and their willingness to take advantage of such opportunities, a model that is based on the chance of economic improvement as assessed by an outside investigator is not likely to work well. If persons within a society share a strong common value system, including possessing similar attitudes toward risk taking (Parsons 1953), then a rational economic model might perform well in the aggregate. However, a premise of this study is that there may be considerable differences in attitudes and perceptions. Such differences are expected to be related to differences among geographical areas that might affect the nature of the socialization of persons from those places.

Many studies of migration in currently developing countries have assumed that differences among origins are unimportant and thus have not considered them (Sabagh 1973). This neglect of origins has been partially due to the difficulty of obtaining data about the characteristics of places of origin for all potential migrants to any given destination. Often migrants are surveyed in a major urban center, and it is logistically difficult to obtain information about the population at places of origin. Many studies have been concerned with planning problems, such as the expected growth of an urban area due to migration in the next ten years (Goldstein 1973b). Such an orientation does not immediately encourage research into the process of selection of migrants among possible origins.

Even when studies in urban areas have been concerned with reasons for migration, the interpretation has often been faulty. Many studies have asked migrants in cities why they came to the city, giving possible choices such as "economic reasons" or "the attraction of the bright lights." Usually the most common reasons have been economic or educational (Simmons, Diaz-Briquets, and Laquian 1977: 51). Some researchers have taken this as confirmation that migration is caused by economic incentives and that differential attitudes toward risk taking or curiosity about different places are unimportant (Byerlee 1972). This is not necessarily the correct interpretation. Even if migrants state that they migrated due to economic reasons, this does not mean that they had any greater potential economic gain from migration than those who remained at the origin. Also, it may be socially more acceptable to state an economic rather than a non-economic reason for migration. A person may think that an economic reason sounds more legitimate than a non-economic reason, which may be construed as frivolous.

In a technical demographic sense, if one wants to study the causes of migration, it is proper to concentrate on the places of origin of migration, since the persons at the origin are the population at risk of migrating (they are the candidates for becoming migrants). Migrants are selected from the origin population rather than from the population at the destination.

A more basic reason for the neglect of origins has been a misinterpretation of the work of the economist, W. Arthur Lewis. Lewis proposed a model of migration intended for application to developing countries in which he assumed there is an unlimited supply of labor ready to work in the modern sector of the economy. He identified modern sector establishments as those whose employment practices were based on achievement rather than ascriptive criteria.[2] Such establishments would hire an additional worker or fire a currently employed worker only if the value of his expected production were greater than or equal to his wage. Such achievement-related employment practices are less common in traditional sector businesses in which persons are rarely

---

[2] Ascriptive characteristics are those that are fixed from birth, such as sex, race, and father's education, or those that automatically change regardless of actions by the individual, such as age. Achievement characteristics are those that it is possible for a person to influence, such as education or a desire to succeed.

fired and others are hired due to kin connections, even if their employment is unprofitable to the establishment.[3] Many traditional sector jobs are not jobs for which one is hired at all but rather are self-created jobs, such as being a self-appointed porter at the bus station or a shoeshiner or pedicab driver. Lewis assumed that there was massive unemployment and underemployment in all parts of the developing country. His model actually referred to economic rather than geographic regions of a country (Lewis 1954).

Some persons have interpreted Lewis's contention that there is essentially an unlimited supply of labor available for modern sector jobs as meaning that there would not exist differences between areas in rates of producing persons seeking such jobs or that any such differences between areas would be unimportant (Todaro 1969: 138-148). This is incorrect. Areas of a country could differ greatly in their rates of production of persons seeking modern sector jobs, and there still could be many more persons seeking modern jobs than there were modern job positions.

Although one part of the development economic theory of migration originated by Lewis and elaborated by others (Todaro 1969; Harris and Todaro 1970; Fields 1975) deals with causes of migration, the other part deals with characteristics of destinations and behavior of migrants upon reaching a destination, especially an urban, relatively industrial destination. The development economic theory contends that those places with the most modern job opportunities should be the major destinations. In general, this is

---

[3] It is not suggested that personal factors are unimportant in obtaining modern sector jobs. The difference suggested is a relative one. Mark Granovetter (1974) found that even for highly technical and managerial jobs in the contemporary United States, personal contacts were extremely important. However, persons were rarely hired unless it seemed that their employment would be profitable to the employer.

probably true, and in a later section on destinations of migration, this contention is examined for Russia in the late nineteenth century.

The differences between areas in rate of production of job seekers are also related to the characteristics of migrants and their ease of adjustment to urban life. Many studies have found that migrants are positively selected according to education or level of skill among all persons at the origin (Long 1973: 243-258; Herrick 1965; Browning and Feindt 1969; Speare 1974) but that they are less advanced in terms of education, skill, or modern attitudes than the natives of the destination, especially if the destination is a major urban, industrial center. The nature of the adaptation of migrants to an urban center in terms of their characteristics has been a major focus of a group of interrelated studies by graduate students and faculty at Brown University (Population Studies and Training Center, Brown University 1978). These studies have generally found that the more educated migrants and those with previous urban experience have adapted more successfully to urban life than those with less education or less urban experience. This might suggest that if a potential migrant has any awareness of this differential ease of adjustment, more educated or skilled migrants might be more willing to attempt urban life than those with lesser educational or skill qualifications.

The concern with selectivity of migrants has usually dealt with differences between individual migrants and non-migrants at the origin (Speare 1974). Rarely has it included a concern with the ecological effects of the social environment at the origin on the propensity to migrate. Where ecological characteristics of origins have been used as variables, they have often been interpreted as surrogates for the individual characteristics of migrants (Levy and Wadycki 1973; Greenwood 1969: 289). For instance, when researchers have found the out-migration rate to a city positively related to the average educational level at the origin, this has usually been interpreted as meaning that the migrants are positively selected according to the possession of a high level of education.

This study does not view origins simply as places that differ in the proportions of persons possessing various characteristics that may individually make them more or less prone to migrate. Nor does it view origins simply as places that differ in opportunities for various types of work and thus vary in the advantage that might accrue to a resident by remaining at the origin as opposed to migrating to a given destination. Rather it conceptualizes the origin as forming the environment in which persons are socialized and in which general attitudes are formed, including attitudes that relate to a person's willingness to migrate to any given destination.

The concern with the characteristics of the places of origin of potential migrants to a given destination reflects an intentional concern with ecological characteristics rather than with the individual characteristics of migrants as compared to non-migrants. There are both practical and theoretical reasons for this concern. Data are much more readily available on ecological characteristics of places than on individuals by migration status by place of origin. Thus scholars are often forced to utilize such data. However, a theoretical concern with the effects of an environment for socialization properly requires the use of ecological data. For instance, in this study, a place with a high literacy rate is not viewed simply as a place whose inhabitants are more likely to be literate than inhabitants of a place with a lower literacy rate. An illiterate person who lives in an area with a high literacy rate is likely to have more information and more accurate information about other places than an illiterate person in an area with a lower literacy rate. The illiterate person in a highly literate area is also likely to be more receptive to new ideas than his counterpart in an area with a lower literacy rate. Similarly, a person who lives in an area where a high proportion of the population is engaged in fairly modern industrial work may be less reluctant to move to an industrial destination than a person in an area where work in industry is rare. Even if an individual has never held an industrial job, if many persons in the area in which he lives hold industrial jobs, he is more likely to be acquainted with someone who has held an industrial job and to be less daunted by the prospect of migrating to an area where industrial work is common than is a person from an area where work in industry is rare.

Of course a concern with ecological characteristics of origins does not mean that individual characteristics are unimportant. Rather, it is likely that both of these kinds of characteristics affect behavior. And although it has often been assumed that only individual characteristics matter, when ecological characteristics have been separated from individual characteristics in other studies of demographic behavior, it has sometimes appeared that the ecological characteristics were more important than the individual characteristics. A study of human fertility in Russia in 1926 (Coale, Anderson, and Härm 1979) found that provinces in which a large proportion of the population were not Great Russians had lower marital fertility than provinces where the population was almost exclusively Great Russian. However, in the provinces with a substantial proportion of non-Great Russians, Great Russians had as low or lower marital fertility on average as non-Great Russians. This could not be explained by differences in female literacy between Great Russians in primarily Great Russian and in heavily non-Great Russian provinces. Rather, the most likely explanation seemed to be that areas with large numbers of non-Great Russians had a cultural (normative) environment that facilitated low marital fertility for Great Russians and non-Great Russians alike.

Kingsley Davis has proposed a theory of demographic change during modernization called "multiphasic demographic response" (Davis 1963). Davis's theory differs substantially from traditional demographic transition theory (Notestein 1945, Coale 1973). Whereas both theories deal with population behavior after declining mortality levels during modernization have caused increased rates of population growth, demographic transition theory is mainly concerned with reductions in fertility, through the eventual voluntary control of marital fertility, to the point where fertility and mortality balance, resulting in no or slow population growth. Davis also contends that another population strategy to decrease the growth rate is for persons to migrate out of the rapidly growing area. It is his belief that migration as a population response has been insufficiently considered by earlier researchers.

One problem with Davis's theory is that it does not specify which situations should lead to fertility reduction and which situations should produce out-migration as a demographic response. Generally, partial tests of Davis's theory have examined countries with or without high rates of migration from rural areas to urban centers. Fertility reduction in the rural areas has been expected in those cases without high migration rates to urban areas, while fertility reduction has not been expected to occur when an urban center absorbs a great deal of the rural population. The results of these partial tests have been mixed (Friedlander 1969; Chamratrithrung 1976; Mosher 1978).

It is possible that the researchers wishing to test Davis's theory have considered the wrong kinds of migration as a possible response to population pressure. If the conceptualization that this study offers is valid, then an available agricultural frontier would be much more attractive to victims of population pressure than a modernizing urban area. By studying out-migration generally or migration to urban areas specifically, migration to an agricultural frontier may have been overlooked. If a person decided to migrate due to population pressure at his origin, he would not necessarily be motivated by a desire to take risks. Therefore, he might well be attracted to a destination as similar to his origin as possible (an agricultural area) but without the problem that he encountered at his origin of too many people for the available resources. In an agricultural frontier destination a person could pursue farming in a manner that he was accustomed to but where adequate land was available for his needs.

When this research was originally planned, it was expected that there would be substantial differences between the characteristics of origins of migrants to an agricultural frontier (Asiatic Russia) as compared to the origins of those who migrated to major urban and industrial centers (Moscow and St. Petersburg cities). The cities were culturally and industrially modern, while the agricultural frontier exhibited few modern characteristics. Originally there was no explicit hypothesis concerning the modernity of origin of migrants who went to destinations that were intermediate in modernity between Asiatic Russia and the two great cities. However, in the course of the research, it was apparent that destinations that were intermediate in modernity between the two great cities and Asiatic Russia drew migrants from origins that were also intermediate in modernity between the origins of migrants to Asiatic Russia and the origins of migrants to Moscow and St. Petersburg cities. Thus a hierarchy of destinations was identified in which the characteristics of origins of migrants to a particular destination differed according to the relative modernity of the particular destination among all major destinations. For example, migration within European Russia, where the destination was neither the great cities of Moscow or St. Petersburg nor the major mining areas in the Urals or the Donbass, showed a pattern of origins intermediate between the pattern of origins of migrants to Moscow or St. Petersburg and the pattern of origins of migrants to Asiatic Russia. Thus the original dichotomous conceptualization of types of destinations proved to be the extreme points in a more finely graded ordering of types of destinations.

This hierarchy may be considered in terms of Samuel Stouffer's theory of intervening opportunities. Stouffer wrote that "the number of persons going a given distance is directly proportional to the number of opportunities at that distance and inversely proportional to the number of intervening opportunities" (Stouffer 1940: 845-924). Opportunities have been variously defined, but essentially Stouffer suggests that a person will choose destination A rather than destination B if A and B are equally attractive but A is closer than B to his place of origin. Although Stouffer formulated his theory in terms of physical distance, it can be reformulated in terms of social distance. In this case, migrants from a moderately modern origin might tend to choose destinations that were more modern than their origin but not necessarily the most modern destination, if there were a destination of intermediate modernity available. A similar idea is stage migration, in which migrants move from rural areas to regional urban centers and then on to national urban centers. In her study of Surabaya, Indonesia, a regional urban center, Laurie McCutcheon (1977) found evidence of earlier migrants to Surabaya moving on to Jakarta.

The discovery of this hierarchy of patterns of origins according to the level and type of modernization of the destination was not expected at the inception of this research. However, once it emerged, it was immediately recognized as consistent with the study's original model. Thus after migration to the major modern destinations (Moscow and St. Petersburg) and the major agricultural frontier destinations (Siberia and northern Central Asia) are investigated, destinations with intermediate characteristics will be examined (Ural and Donbass mining areas and European Russia other than Moscow or St. Petersburg cities, the Urals, or the Donbass).

Comparable variables are used in the analysis throughout the study. In each case, the research employs an agricultural variable, a culturable modernization variable, an industrial modernization variable, and a population pressure variable. Where appropriate, a variable reflecting the difficulty of getting from the origin to the potential destination (a kind of distance variable) is used. Occasionally the research considers other variables. The specific choice of variables is discussed in the next chapter. The model tested in this research is illustrated schematically in Figure 1.1 and also in the Summary of Hypotheses on page 21.

Characteristics of Origin	Less Modern Destination	More Modern Destination
Importance of Traditional Agriculture	+	−
Cultural Modernity	−	+
Industrial Modernity	−	+
Population Pressure	+	−

FIGURE 1.1 Schematic Representation of the Pattern of Explanatory Variables According to the Modernity of the Destination of Migration.

SUMMARY OF HYPOTHESES

HYPOTHESES FOR MIGRATION WITHIN A SETTLED AREA

1. Migration rates are positively related to the cultural modernization of the place of origin.
2. Migration rates are positively related to the industrial modernization of the place of origin.
3. Migration rates are not strongly positively related to population pressure at the origin and thus are not mainly determined by such pressure.
4. Migration rates are negatively related to the importance of traditional agriculture at the origin.
5. Migration rates to specific destinations decrease with increasing difficulty of reaching the destination.

HYPOTHESES FOR MIGRATION TO A FRONTIER AREA

6. Migration rates are negatively related to the cultural modernization of the origin.
7. Migration rates are negatively related to the industrial modernization of the origin.
8. Migration rates are positively related to the importance of traditional agriculture at the origin.
9. Population pressure is strongly positively related to migration rates and is a main determinant of such rates.
10. If migration to a frontier area begins at a definite date, then over time hypotheses 6-9 are increasingly more strongly supported.
11. Migration rates decrease with increasing difficulty of reaching the destination.

HYPOTHESES CONCERNING RELATIVE DISTRIBUTION OF
MIGRANTS AMONG DESTINATIONS

12. The differences between characteristics of origins of migrants to settled destinations and to frontier destinations

are also expected to appear in the relative distribution of migrants between the two types of destinations.

13. On balance, the migration rates out of origins are generally expected to more closely resemble the pattern hypothesized for migration within a settled area than hypothesized for migration to a frontier area.

HYPOTHESES ABOUT CHARACTERISTICS OF MIGRANTS

14. Migrants have more modern or more skilled characteristics than non-migrants.

CHAPTER 2

Russia as a Modernizing Society at the End of the Nineteenth Century

BACKGROUND

The previous chapter discussed the characteristics of a modernizing society. This chapter presents evidence which demonstrates that late nineteenth-century European Russia was a modernizing society and thus is an appropriate case for investigation of the proposed model. In addition, this chapter also provides a background for understanding the major explanatory variables and the particular destinations studied.

There are several traditionally important areas and cities in Russian society whose locations are shown on Map 2.1. Since these areas and cities are discussed throughout this research, it will be helpful to the reader if he keeps their locations in mind. On all subsequent maps, Moscow City and St. Petersburg City are designated M and P, respectively. Map A.1, in the appendix, gives province names.

The exact extent of the Ukraine is a matter of disagreement. Therefore, Map 2.1 shows this area according to two different definitions. One definition corresponds to Soviet demographer V. M. Kabuzan's (1971: 174-175) use of nineteenth-century administrative boundaries; the other corresponds to the limits of the present Ukrainian S.S.R. and Moldavian S.S.R. (Lydolph 1970: 94-98). In this study, I found it unnecessary to treat the Ukraine as a special area according to either definition. Rather, the behavior of persons born in the Ukraine was adequately explained through

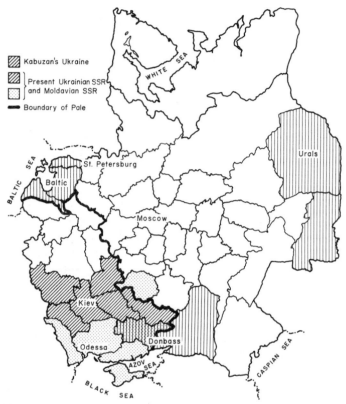

MAP 2.1   Major Areas and Cities

the use of ordinary socio-economic variables without the necessity of taking into account the existence of the Ukraine as a distinct cultural area.

Map 2.1 also indicates the extent of the Pale. Jews who had less than a certain amount of education or who were not in certain high status occupations were legally required to live in the Pale, a requirement that affected the vast majority of Jews (Dubnow 1975: II, 343). As shown on the map, neither Moscow nor St. Petersburg cities were located in this area. Since Odessa and Kiev were the largest cities within the Pale, the proportion Jewish in the province of birth or alternatively the location of the province of birth within the Pale is a major consideration in examination of migration to those cities. Although both Kiev and Odessa were in the Pale, there were restrictions on the residence of Jews in Kiev, while there were no such restrictions in Odessa. The effects of this legal distinction are also found to be important in determining migration to the two cities.

The provinces of most intense mining activity in European Russia were in the Urals or the Don Basin (also called Donbass) and are indicated on the map. These provinces also included some of the last remaining arable land in European Russia to be subjected to cultivation. In this research, the designated provinces in the Urals and the Donbass will be considered separately as destinations.

The three Baltic provinces were quite different from the rest of European Russia: non-Slavic languages were spoken there, and the predominant religion was Lutheran rather than Russian Orthodox. These provinces later became Estonia and Latvia. As has been common in other studies of European Russia as a social system (Coale, Anderson, and Härm 1979), the three Baltic provinces were excluded from the list of considered origins. Also excluded from the list of provinces considered as places of origin are provinces that included the major destinations studied in detail (Moscow and St. Petersburg, the two Ural provinces, and the two Donbass provinces).[1]

[1] The three Baltic provinces are extreme outliers for many relations, and thus their inclusion would distort many of the relations studied. For migration within European Russia generally, the Baltic provinces are included as destinations, since test runs showed that this inclusion had little effect on the results. The only province with a substantial amount of migration to the Baltic provinces was Kovno, which later became

Comparison of results for migration to different destinations requires that the set of provinces considered as origins be identical. For the remainder of this chapter, when information is presented that bears on the characteristics of the provinces of European Russia considered as places of origin, the data are shown for the forty-one provinces of birth not excluded for the above reasons. At times, information is given intended simply to portray the general characteristics of European Russia. In such cases, data may be presented for all fifty provinces of this area.

AGRICULTURE

European Russia demonstrated great diversity in climatic and soil conditions. Map 2.2 shows agricultural areas defined by type of soil, predominant vegetation, and precipitation level (Lydolph 1970: 15-23). In some countries, such as France, such a coarse geographic division would make little sense, particularly if there were great variability in soil and climate conditions within a small area such that any such averaged representation of conditions would be far from the actual situation for many local areas. In Russia, however, due to the general flatness of the land and the predominant lack of great variations in soil or climate within small areas, conditions of soil and climate are fairly homogeneous within any one province, and thus the aver-

---

Lithuania. Exclusion of Kovno from the set of origins was considered because it also differed noticeably from the rest of European Russia. However, the differences were not as extreme as for the three provinces that later became Estonia and Latvia. Kovno was predominantly Roman Catholic rather than Protestant, and literacy was not as high as in the three Baltic provinces. Also Kovno was not usually an outlier and thus would not have distorted the relationships obtained from the other provinces.

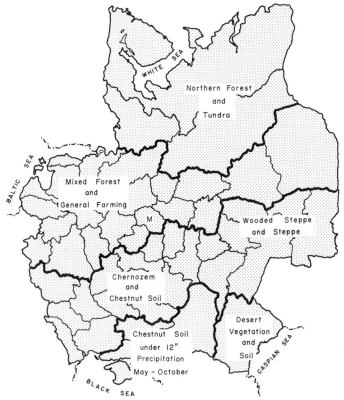

MAP 2.2   Agricultural Areas

age conditions for the province are fairly representative of all places within that province (Parker 1969: 27).

Map 2.3 shows a division of the country into five levels of soil fertility. This is de Tegoborskii's (1972: I, 30) system, which is based generally on climate and type of soil. That differences in the nature of soil among areas in Russia have long been recognized is indicated by the prevalence in the literature and other writings of terms such as "black soil area" and "chestnut soil area."

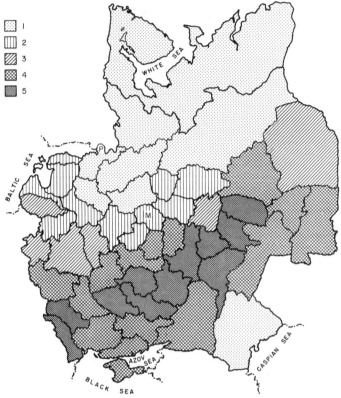

MAP 2.3   Level of Soil Fertility

These differences in soil and climate were related to the nature of work organization in premodern and early modern Russia. In the northern area, where the soil fertility level is generally low, the cold climate prevented the profitable pursuit of agriculture in the winter. By contrast, in the higher soil fertility area in the south, the climate was sufficiently mild for the growing of crops throughout the year. The southern province of Astrakhan is assigned a low soil fertility level not due to cold but rather due to the extreme aridity of the soil.

Due to these geographic differences cottage industries were long common in the north, while their pursuit was more infrequent in the south. By 1800, the differences in conditions of agriculture throughout the year had led to a geographic difference in the manner in which serfs satisfied their obligation to their owners (Blum 1961: 394-397). In the north, where the soil fertility level was low, a quitrent system, called *obrok*, was common. In this system, a serf paid a certain amount of money to his owner each year. This money could be obtained by selling crops at market, from the sale of goods produced in cottage industry, or through wages obtained in industry or agricultural work done in other areas. Since it was in the owner's interest to facilitate the accumulation of money by his serfs, owners in the north were often willing to allow their serfs to pursue wage labor jobs in the winter. In the south, where agricultural labor could be profitably employed throughout the year, the usual system by which a serf satisfied his obligation to his owner was through farm labor. In this system, called *barschina*, a serf was obligated to work up to three days a week on the owner's land. Thus even before substantial industrialization had occurred in European Russia, there was a noticeable difference among areas in the proportion of the population whose economic support was obtained solely from traditional agriculture. When industry developed, persons in the north were more likely than those in the south to engage at least in seasonal wage work.

In 1897, over half of the population in each of the forty-one provinces of origin considered obtained their primary support from agriculture, fishing, or forestry. On the average, over 75 percent of the population of these forty-one provinces obtained economic support mainly from these primary industrial activities. However, many persons whose support was primarily from agriculture also had an auxiliary source of support, such as cottage industry or seasonal wage work. This pattern of auxiliary employment of those primarily in agriculture was strongly related to soil fertility.

Table 2.1 shows the correlations among the three types of agricultural variables: soil fertility, percentage of serfs on *obrok* in the 1850s, and percentage of those primarily in agriculture who had an auxiliary occupation in 1897.[2] The *obrok* variable refers to privately owned estate serfs. Approximately half of the serfs in the 1850s were owned by the state (Kabuzan 1971), and virtually all state serfs were on

TABLE 2.1

CORRELATIONS AMONG VARIOUS AGRICULTURAL VARIABLES

	Soil Fertility	% on Obrok 1850s	% with Aux Occ 1897
Soil	1.000	-.642 (36)	-.554 (41)
% on Obrok 1850s		1.000	.638 (36)
% with Aux Occ 1897			1.000

NOTE: p <.001 for all correlation coefficients, two-tailed tests. Number of cases on which correlations are computed appear in parentheses.

[2] A correlation measures the extent to which two variables vary together. It ranges from -1 to $+1$. The larger the absolute value of the correlation, the greater the relationship in the variation of the two variables. A high positive correlation means that high values for one variable generally accompany high values for the other variable. A strong negative correlation means that one variable usually has a high value when the other variable has a low value. A correlation near zero means that there is no general relationship between the two variables. The correlation is a standardized measure of association, so that adding a number to one variable (for all cases) or multiplying one variable by a constant (for all cases) does not affect the correlation of that variable with any other variable. A significance test is termed two-tailed if the magnitude of the coefficient is compared to zero. A significance test is termed one-tailed if the coefficient is compared only to possible values greater than zero or less than zero. Thus a two-tailed test is a stricter test than a one-tailed test.

the *obrok* system. State serfs were a larger proportion of the serf population in the north than in the south. The *obrok* data were available only for forty-two out of the fifty provinces of European Russia. Data were available for only thirty-six out of the forty-one provinces considered as provinces of births in this study. The pattern of correlations shown in Table 2.1 is as expected: the higher the soil fertility, the lower the proportion on *obrok* before emancipation of the serfs and the lower the proportion of those in agriculture who had an auxiliary occupation in 1897.

Table 2.2 shows the mean and standard deviation of the *obrok* and auxiliary industry variables within each level of soil fertility for those of the forty-one provinces of interest for which data were available.[3] The frequency of both *obrok*

TABLE 2.2

PERCENTAGE ON OBROK IN THE 1850S AND PERCENTAGE WITH AN AUXILIARY OCCUPATION IN 1897 BY LEVEL OF SOIL FERTILITY

	(lower)		Level of Soil Fertility	(higher)	
	1	2	3	4	5
% Estate Peasants on Obrok in 1850s					
Mean	48	52	15	12	14
s.d.	23	22	17	11	14
n	(6)	(5)	(5)	(10)	(10)
% of those Primarily in Agriculture with an Auxiliary Occupation in 1897					
Mean	36	31	19	18	19
s.d.	15	15	14	5	2
n	(7)	(7)	(5)	(11)	(11)

[3] The mean of a variable is the average value it attains over the cases considered. The standard deviation (s.d.) is a measure of the spread of a variable about its mean. The larger the standard deviation, the greater the extent to which the values of the variable are widely dispersed about the mean.

and auxiliary employment generally decreases as soil fertility increases. However, for both variables, there is a definite difference between soil fertility levels 1-2 and soil fertility levels 3-5. Since this difference is so marked, later analyses occasionally compare a low soil fertility group of provinces (those at soil fertility levels 1-2) with a high soil fertility group of provinces (those at soil fertility levels 3-5).

Since the vast majority of the population in most provinces engaged primarily in agriculture or similar primary industrial activities such as fishing or forestry, the proportion of the population in agriculture did not seem a sufficiently differentiating variable to indicate the level of intensity of involvement in agriculture in a province. However, the soil fertility variable did seem appropriate since there was very little technical improvement in agriculture outside of the Baltic in the nineteenth century (Parker 1969: 27; Volin 1970: 61-65). The strong relationship of soil fertility with the variables relating to work organization in Tables 2.1 and 2.2 also supports the appropriateness of the interpretation of the soil fertility variable. For these reasons, this study uses the soil fertility variable to indicate the intensity of involvement in agriculture. Many analyses in this research were repeated using the auxiliary occupation variable or the proportion of the population in agriculture as the agricultural indicator. Since these substitutions made no substantial difference in the findings, the following discussion presents only the results for the soil fertility variable.

LITERACY

Literacy was increasing rapidly in late nineteenth-century European Russia. Figure 2.1 (Rashin 1956: 305-306) graphs the percentage of military recruits who were literate at three dates. This is shown for forty-one provinces (Baltic

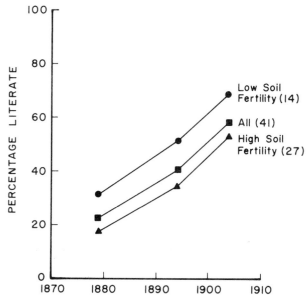

FIGURE 2.1 Percentage of Military Recruits Literate, 1874-1883, 1894 and 1904 by Level of Soil Fertility

provinces, Moscow and St. Petersburg provinces, Urals and Donbass provinces excluded) and also for two divisions according to the level of soil fertility. Soil fertility levels 1-2 are grouped together into a low soil fertility group, and soil fertility levels 3-5 are combined into a high soil fertility group. In each case, the increase in literacy over time reflects the overall process of societal development. The figure also reveals consistently higher literacy of the low soil fertility area, even though the highly literate Baltic provinces and Moscow and St. Petersburg are omitted.

The increasing literacy of the European Russian population in the late nineteenth century is also suggested by the percentage of rural females by age group who were literate according to the 1897 census (Rashin 1956: 293). Table 2.3

demonstrates a steady decrease in the proportion literate with increasing age. Women not literate by their early twenties usually remained illiterate throughout their lives.[4] Thus the data in Table 2.3 suggest that in the last half of the nineteenth century, literacy was becoming more common, even among rural females.

TABLE 2.3

PERCENTAGE OF EUROPEAN RUSSIAN RURAL FEMALES WHO
WERE LITERATE BY AGE GROUP: 1897

Age Group	% Literate
10-19	17
20-29	15
30-39	12
40-49	9
50-59	8
60+	7

[4] In a study of human fertility in Russia (Coale, Anderson, and Härm 1979), literacy of the rural population of European Russia by province in 1897 was compared to the proportion literate of the same sex and comparable age group in 1926 (that is, those aged twenty to twenty-four in 1897 were compared to those aged fifty to fifty-four in 1926). It was found that for rural females, the percentage literate for the two dates was virtually unchanged province by province when the age in 1897 was at least twenty. For males in general, there was a substantial increase in literacy between 1897 and 1926, possibly due to military service. For these reasons, it seems plausible to interpret rural female proportions literate by age as indicating proportions becoming literate by their twenties; such an interpretation might not be valid for male literacy rates by age. Although there was a similar decrease in literacy with age for males (although a higher percentage of males than females literate for each age group), the female literacy data seemed sounder evidence for a general increase in literacy than did the male evidence. Note that while changing standards of selection into military service (changing ease of getting out of service) might affect the pattern of literacy of military recruits, there is not a similar problem for literacy of rural females. Also the effect of migration on the rural female literacy variable would generally be to depress the meas-

Literacy is the cultural variable used in this analysis of migration, as it has been found by other researchers to be a good indicator of cultural modernization (Goldstein 1973a). Other possibilities would include measures of human fertility or urbanization. Literacy, however, is more likely to be directly tied to information than are the birth rate or the percentage urban. It is also more directly related to Black's definition of modernization in terms of knowledge than are the other possibilities.

Literacy of military recruits 1874-1883 provided an attractive literacy variable for analysis, since this was the first date for which fairly comparable literacy data across all provinces of European Russia were available. The first date for which the literacy of the total population was available was 1897, but it is preferable for explanatory variables to predate the time of measurement of the dependent variables.

As was the case for most European countries in the nineteenth century, Russian military recruits did not volunteer for service. Rather they were selected through a draft system that persons generally wished to avoid (Blum 1961: 465-468; Florinsky 1953: II, 906-909). Thus the average literacy of military recruits may not have been identical to the average literacy of the adult or adult male population of the province from which they were recruited. However, if the relationship between literacy of military recruits and literacy of others in that province did not systematically vary across provinces in a manner related to migration, then the pattern of the relationship of migration to literacy would be unaffected.[5]

---

ured proportion literate in the younger age groups since the volume of migration had increased and migration was likely to have been selective of the more literate, younger women.

[5] Note that the statistical tests of relationships used in this study (correlations, partial correlations, and standardized regression coefficients are

Map 2.4 shows the percentage of military recruits who were literate 1874-1883. The areas of high literacy were near Moscow and the Baltic area as well as in the far south. It is apparent that literacy was generally negatively related to soil fertility. For forty-one provinces, the correlation between the literacy of these military recruits and soil fertility is $-.609$.

One mechanism that may partially account for the relationship between literacy and soil fertility is the greater frequency of seasonal industrial work in the northern area of lower soil fertility. Von Laue (1961) presents evidence that workers in factories often became literate while working. Tugan-Baranovskii (1900) attributes the extremely high level of literacy in Yaroslavl province to the frequency of seasonal wage work in that province. The markedly high literacy level in Yaroslavl is apparent on Map 2.4.

Literacy of the resident population of provinces in 1897 would be affected by migration before 1897 and might not accurately reflect the literacy level of natives of one province relative to natives of other provinces. There is some reason to believe that the effect of migration on literacy relations among provinces might be substantial. The correlation between literacy of military recruits 1874-1883 and the percentage of the resident population of provinces in 1897 who were literate is only .529. However, among the twenty-

---

sensitive only to the pattern of relationships among variables and not to the absolute level of the variables (see note 2). Thus even if military recruits were more or less literate than others of the same age, if there were no systematic relationship across provinces between the difference between the literacy of recruits and the literacy of natives of the province, then the statistical results would be unbiased. Random deviations in the relationship between literacy of recruits and natives would simply act as "noise" and would generally weaken the strength of the measured relationships between literacy and other variables.

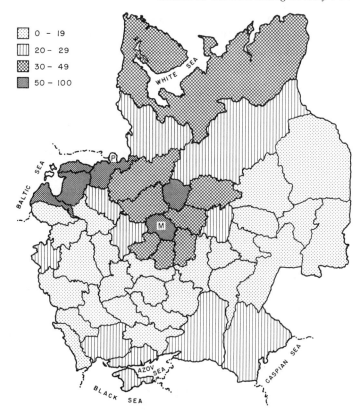

MAP 2.4   Percentage Military Recruits Literate: 1874-1883

three provinces (out of the forty-one provinces) where at least 95 percent of the residents in 1897 were natives of the province, the correlation was .862. For the other eighteen provinces where less than 95 percent of the resident population were natives of the province, the correlation was only .548. This is what would be expected if the literacy rate of migrants were substantially different from that of non-migrants.

The question of the relationship of migration of literate

persons to migration from highly literate provinces is discussed in the chapter on migration to Moscow and St. Petersburg cities.

FERTILITY, MORTALITY, AND NATURAL INCREASE

Throughout the nineteenth century, the rate of natural increase (natural r) of the population rose slowly, due to a more rapid general decline in mortality than in fertility. Figure 2.2 shows the crude birth rate, the crude death rate, and the rate of natural increase of the European Russian population by single years 1861-1910 (Rashin 1956: 155-

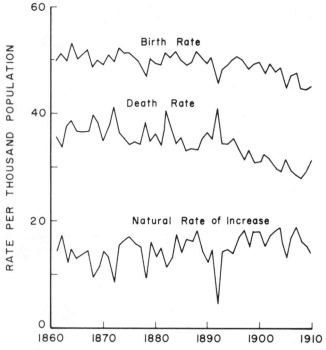

FIGURE 2.2 Crude Demographic Rates for European Russia: 1861-1910

156).[6] Data for 1866 were not available. Although mortality conditions were generally improving, there were large year-to-year fluctuations. The effects of famines in southern Russia in 1891 and 1901 can be seen on the figure. With modernization, mortality usually declines, as it did in European Russia. Sometime later, fertility generally declines, eventually through voluntary control of marital fertility. Among rural areas in 1897, only the Baltic provinces displayed evidence of voluntary control of marital fertility. Generally, differences in the age of female marriage were the major source of interprovincial differences in rural fertility levels (Coale, Anderson, and Härm 1979).

Many economists who have studied migration have maintained that "population pressure" forces persons in modernizing societies to move out of agricultural origins. In general, discussions of population pressure do not define specifically what is meant by this term (Simmons, Diaz-Briquets, and Laquian 1977: 46, 51). The gist of it, though, is that the increase in population over time causes a shortage of resources per capita or a general dissatisfaction with crowding (Boserup 1970). Kingsley Davis's (1963) theory of multiphasic demographic response also posits migration as an outlet for population pressure alternative to reduced fertility.

Some researchers have used an estimate of the "carrying

[6] The crude birth rate is the number of persons born in a year to a population per thousand persons in that population. Similarly, the crude death rate is the number of persons in a population who die in a year per thousand persons in that population. The rate of natural increase is the crude birth rate minus the crude death rate and is thus the number of persons by which a population grows per thousand population due only to fertility and mortality. These measures can be computed for periods other than one year by taking the births (or deaths or difference between births and deaths) per thousand population and then dividing by the number of years in the period under consideration.

capacity" of the land as an indicator of population pressure. This has sometimes been operationally defined as the ratio of non-city population to cultivated farm area (Mendoza-Pascual 1966). Since Russia was predominantly rural in the late nineteenth century, this measure would be similar to the density of the population. A common problem with density and with carrying capacity is that the nature of agricultural conditions determines whether a given density (carrying capacity) is too high. Density would also be affected by other aspects of land use. The population growth rate, a second common indicator of population pressure, would also not be a good choice, since it is influenced by migration. As there was very little technical improvement in agriculture before 1900 outside the Baltic (Parker 1969: 27) and as the rate of natural increase reflects the extent to which an area becomes more crowded with time apart from the influence of migration, the rate of natural increase seemed the best available candidate for an indicator of population pressure.

In this study, natural r 1881-1885 is used to indicate the level of population pressure. Map 2.5 shows natural r 1881-1885. Most of the migration data analyzed in this study refer to lifetime migration as assessed by place of residence in 1897 compared to place of birth. The period 1881-1885 was chosen as the time frame in which to measure natural r, since it was somewhat before 1897 and might approximate the time at which many persons defined as lifetime migrants in 1897 actually moved.

These years were not a particularly unusual time period for natural r. Table 2.10 shows correlations among the explanatory variables used in this study. It also includes correlations with natural r for other time periods in the late nineteenth and early twentieth centuries. It is clear that 1881-1885 was not a particularly abnormal period to pick, since the correlations between natural r 1881-1885 and the

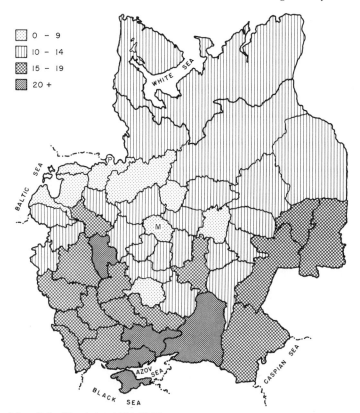

0 – 9
10 – 14
15 – 19
20 +

MAP 2.5   Natural r: 1881-1885

literacy, agricultural, and industrial variables are quite similar to those among these other explanatory variables and natural r for other time periods. On the other hand, natural r 1891-1895 would not have been a good indicator of population pressure generally, since during this time period natural r departed considerably from its typical pattern. This deviation is revealed by the quite different correlations between natural r 1891-1895 and the other explanatory variables as compared to the pattern among the explanatory variables and natural r for other time periods.[7] A severe famine in 1891-1892 considerably affected the pattern of natural r. Its major effect was to decrease natural r in the south through a substantial increase in the death rate. The effects of this famine are discussed in more detail in the chapter on migration to Asiatic Russia.

Many parts of the analysis substituted population density or the growth rate as the indicator of the level of population pressure. However, these differences in the indicator had no substantial effect on the results.

DISTANCE

Like most other studies of migration, this study employs a distance measure. It serves essentially as a correction factor so that the "true" relation between migration propensity and explanatory variables can be detected. Measures of distance are thought to incorporate both the economic and psychological costs of moving (Isard 1960: 493-568). Some researchers have used indirect measures of distance, such as travel time or airline fare. The correlations between the measures of distance used in this study and the explanatory variables are shown in Table 2.10

It is clear that the distribution of the explanatory variables is not unrelated to the distance to various destinations. For instance, the correlation between literacy of military recruits 1874-1883 and the measure of distance to St. Petersburg City is − .406. Provinces close to St. Petersburg

---

[7] The correlation of natural r 1881-1885 with the natural logarithm of the distance to Asiatic Russia in hundreds of miles does differ from the correlation of that distance measure with natural r in other time periods. The possible effect of this difference in the relationship of natural r 1881-1885 to distance as compared to other time periods on the results for migration to Asiatic Russia is examined in the chapter on Asiatic Russia.

generally had a higher percentage of military recruits literate than provinces that were more distant from St. Petersburg. Even if persons migrated randomly but tended to travel only a certain maximal distance from their origin, one might observe a positive relationship between the literacy of the province of birth and the migration rate to St. Petersburg City. Thus the relationship between the distance between the origin and destination and the migration rate must be taken into account in order to assess the relationship between other explanatory variables and migration rates apart from the mechanical effects resulting from the geographical distribution of the explanatory variables.

Attitudes relevant to this study can also diffuse from a center of innovation, with the distance from that center thus indicating the strength of the attitude that has diffused. For instance, a willingness to take risks and to be amenable to new ideas might diffuse, and it is probable that such attitudes are positively related to the recognition of the importance of literacy. Thus it is possible that a willingness to take risks diffused from St. Petersburg and the general Baltic area and that this adventuresome spirit was related to the pattern of literacy near the Baltic. In such a case, statistically controlling for the distance from the Baltic would control not only for the mechanical effects of the distribution of literacy discussed earlier but would also, to some extent, control for the strength of willingness to take risks and accept new ideas. There is no direct method of separating the mechanical effects of geographical distribution of a given explanatory variable from the diffusion of attitudes that are of interest to this study if such attitudes are not directly measured. Thus this study takes the conservative approach of attributing differences that may be accounted for by distance as being due to the mechanical effects of geographical distribution.

Throughout this work, the natural logarithm of the distance between the origin and the destination in hundreds of miles is used as the usual distance measure. The natural logarithm of distance increases less rapidly than distance itself. Thus the difference between 1,000 and 1,200 miles is not considered as great as the difference between 100 and 300 miles. It seemed reasonable that increments in distance should become less important the greater the total distance.

INDUSTRY

The belief that Russia did not really begin to industrialize until 1900 or 1917 is countered by available data (Grossman 1973). One of the most important aspects of modernization is economic development through industrialization. Thus it is important to establish that by the end of the nineteenth century, European Russia was an industrializing society.[8]

Simon Kuznets (1966) has noted that if one considers the economy divided into the three sectors, industry, agriculture, and service, then one of the most striking changes with economic development is the increase in the productivity, and usually the share of the labor force, in the industrial sector. These increases are especially marked in manufacturing. Figure 2.3 shows the number of workers in industry per thousand population for 1815-1900 (Rashin 1940: 41, 128; Rashin 1956: 28-29, 44-45). These data are presented for all fifty provinces of European Russia in order to show its general industrial development. The data are also presented for the forty-one provinces considered as origins in this study,

[8] Industrialization is typically an important component of economic development, although there are cases where the development of agriculture has been quite important, perhaps more important (at least in some periods of development) than industrialization. Denmark and France are often cited as examples of the importance of agricultural development (Kuznets 1966).

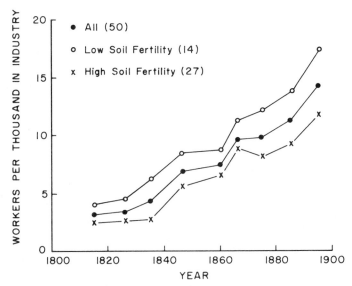

FIGURE 2.3 Workers in Industry Per Thousand Population: 1815-1900
by Level of Soil Fertility (all 50 provinces)

NOTE: After 1860, data are averaged on ten-year intervals

divided into the high soil fertility provinces with soil fertility levels 3-5 and the low soil fertility provinces with soil
fertility levels 1-2. At each date, the low soil fertility provinces had a higher proportion of the population working in
industry than did the high soil fertility provinces. Inclusion
of Moscow and St. Petersburg provinces would have made
the differences between the two soil fertility groups even
greater. This difference in involvement of the population in
industry by soil fertility level is consistent with the earlier
discussion of soil fertility and traditional work organization.
The rapid rises in the proportion of the population in industry generally supports the view of European Russia as industrializing throughout the nineteenth century.

In 1842, British bans on the export of modern spinning

machines were lifted, and shortly thereafter, such machines began to be imported into European Russia (Blackwell 1970: 12; Yatsunsky 1974). While there are those that might suppose that this introduction of spinning machines at such an early date would have little substantial effect even within the Russian cotton industry, this supposition can be disproved. Figure 2.4 graphs imports of raw and spun cotton for 1812-1860 in thousands of poods. A pood is a unit of weight equal to thirty-six pounds (Rashin 1940: 29). It is apparent that while imports of raw cotton increased throughout the period, imports of spun cotton had begun to decrease by 1846-1850. The most obvious explanation of this difference in the pattern of importation of raw and spun cotton is that there was not as great a need to import spun cotton once a sufficient number of efficient spinning machines had been put into production domestically. By 1850, Russia had become the world's fifth largest producer of cotton goods (Blackwell 1970: 13). Thus at least in one part of the economy, the effects of modern machinery were noticeable as early as the 1840s. This was also the argument pre-

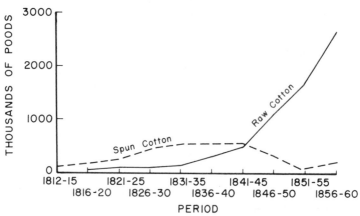

FIGURE 2.4 Imports of Raw and Spun Cotton: 1812-1860

sented by the Soviet economic demographer, A. G. Rashin, from whose book the data in Figure 2.4 were obtained.

Russia was similar to currently developing countries and different from western European countries in her reliance on heavy utilization of imported rather than indigenously developed technology in other industries as well as in the cotton industry (Blackwell 1970: 39-41; Black et al. 1975). Thus in Russia, just as in currently developing countries and unlike the early modernizers in Western Europe and the United States, rapid socio-economic changes precipitated by imported technology were common. Like Russia, many other countries have first seen the effects of modern machinery in the textile industries (Marczewski 1963: 123-130; Tsuru 1963: 149-150).

Nineteenth-century Russian industries can be roughly classified as employing relatively modern manufacturing processes or relatively non-modern manufacturing processes, according to the commodity produced. The less modern processes were usually employed by small enterprises, often run by a single family, while the more modern processes frequently occurred in fairly large factories. Figure 2.5 shows the number of workers in thousands in various industries 1865-1890 (Rashin 1940: 104), classified according to whether the manufacturing process was relatively modern. The graph clearly shows that industries employing relatively modern manufacturing processes were increasing in number of workers more rapidly than those that employed less modern manufacturing processes (Blackwell 1970: 12-14; de Tegoborskii 1972: II, 86-89). At the end of the nineteenth century, the Russian chemical industry has been characterized as primitive, but it only appears primitive when compared to the chemical industry in Western Europe at that time; it was not primitive when compared with Russian methods of manufacture of linen or wool.

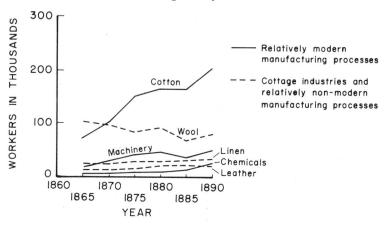

FIGURE 2.5 Workers in Selected Industries: 1865-1890

THE CENSUS CATEGORY "WORKERS AND SERVANTS"

As Kuznets pointed out, the industrial labor force is especially important in modernization. A somewhat larger group that is also important in development is the wage labor force. During modernization, the proportion of the population working for wages rather than engaging in subsistence activity increases. Fortunately, the 1897 Russian Census presented migration data separately for a group that approximates the wage labor force (Russia 1905b). This aggregate was a broad classification that included most persons who were not engaged in normal farming activity, including industrial workers and servants. Hereafter this group will be referred to generally as workers or worker-servants, for convenience. Table 2.4 shows the various categories of work included in worker and servant occupations. Even in the rural economy category, the types of rural activity pursued are often not normal farming but more specialized activities such as stock breeding. The rural economy category also included wage agricultural labor.

Table 2.5 shows the distribution of persons in European

TABLE 2.4

CATEGORIES OF WORKERS AND SERVANTS IN THE IMPERIAL
RUSSIAN CENSUS: 1897

Workers

   I.   Rural economy, fishing and hunting

       A. Agriculture generally
       B. Stock breeding
       C. Other rural economy other than forestry
       D. Forestry and forest industry
       E. Fishing and hunting

  II.   Mining

 III.   Metal refining

  IV.   Fabrication industry (Secondary industry)

       A. Fabrication of plant material
       B. Fabrication of animal material
       C. Wood products
       D. Metal products
       E. Fabrication of mineral matter, ceramics
       F. Chemical products
       G. Winemaking and brewing
       H. Production of other drinks and fermentation products
       I. Fabrication of vegetable and animal products
       J. Making of tobacco and tobacco products
       K. Printing industry
       L. Instrument production
       M. Jewelry and cultural objects
       N. Clothing production
       O. Building and repair
       P. Production of munitions and ships
       Q. Other fabrication

   V.   Post, telegraph and telephone (Communication)

  VI.   Transportation

       A. Water transport
       B. Railroads
       C. Carriage trade
       D. Other land transport

 VII.   Commerce generally

VIII.   Day laborers and unskilled workers

   Servants

   I. In administrative, judicial, social and class establishments

  II. In plants, factories and farms

 III. Household: doorkeepers, porters, night watchmen, etc.

  IV. Household: cooks, footmen, maids, etc.

Russia and in the Russian Empire generally by sex in the various categories of worker and servant occupations. In Table 2.5, the corresponding category from Table 2.4 is indicated by W for worker jobs and S for servant jobs with the appropriate Roman numeral. Males were over twice as

TABLE 2.5

DISTRIBUTION OF WORKERS AND SERVANTS IN EUROPEAN RUSSIA
AND IN THE RUSSIAN EMPIRE: 1897

	European Russia		Russian Empire	
	Male	Female	Male	Female
Pop. in Thou	45,750	47,693	62,500	63,168
Pop W+S in Thou	4,610	2,200	6,335	2,821
% W+S	10.1%	4.6%	10.1%	4.5%
% Distribution of Workers and Servants				
Sec Ind (WIV)	35.7	14.8	31.8	13.4
Metal (WII+III)	3.0	.4	3.1	.4
Rural (WI)	27.8	25.2	31.1	26.7
Unskilled (WVIII)	10.4	9.4	12.8	10.1
TCC (WV, VI+VII)	10.1	2.3	8.9	2.0
Fact Serv (SII)	3.5	.7	3.2	.7
Adm+SocServ(SI)	2.5	1.0	2.3	.9
HH Serv(SIII+IV)	6.9	46.3	6.8	45.8
Total	99.9%	100.1%	100.0%	100.0%

likely as females to hold worker or servant jobs. (No age breakdowns were available for the migration data, so these percentages refer to the entire population of each sex, including children.) Of those in worker-servant jobs, the distribution by sex was also quite different. Males were much more likely to be in secondary industry than were females, while females were more likely to be household servants.

GEOGRAPHICAL DISTRIBUTION OF CATEGORIES OF WORKERS AND SERVANTS

Map 2.6 shows the number of workers (both sexes combined) in secondary industry per thousand population in 1897. Workers in secondary industry are those engaged in production. The secondary industrial sector is similar to Kuznets's industrial sector, except that those working in service jobs in industrial establishments are included in his

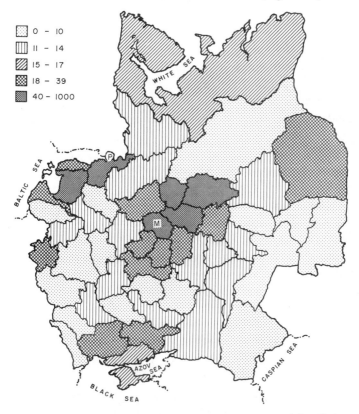

0 – 10	
11 – 14	
15 – 17	
18 – 39	
40 – 1000	

MAP 2.6   Workers in Secondary Industry Per Thousand Population: 1897

classification but not in the secondary industry category. For late nineteenth-century Russia this makes little difference. As shown in Table 2.5, factory servants were a very small percentage of the wage labor force. The operational definition of workers in secondary industry in this study is all occupations appearing in "Fabrication industry" (IV under "Workers" in Table 2.3). "Metal refining" (Workers, III) might have been included in secondary industry but was not because it is so closely related to extractive mining. (This study considers mining a more modern activity than traditional agriculture but less so than secondary industry. The nature of mining activity is discussed in more detail in the chapter on the Urals and the Donbass.) Some cottage industry, such as persons making linen in their backyards, is included in secondary industry as defined. However, in general, modern production methods would have been more commonly utilized in the secondary industrial occupations than in worker-servant occupations in the service sector. Secondary industry was concentrated around Moscow, in the Baltic, and somewhat in the south. The ring of provinces around Moscow was called the "Central Industrial District."

Mining and smelting were concentrated in two areas: in the Urals, especially in Perm and Orenburg provinces, and in the Donets Basin (Donbass), especially in the provinces of Don and Ekaterinslav. Mining was also fairly common in Siberia.

Another important part of the wage labor force are those engaged in commercial activity. This group is similar to Kuznets's service sector. During modernization, this sector changes composition. Traditional service jobs such as hawkers and peddlers or household servants decline in number, while the frequency of more skilled, clerk-type jobs increases. By excluding from the service sector those servants in establishments and households, we are left with workers in commerce, communication, and transportation. Such more modern service workers were relatively numerous in Moscow and St. Petersburg and through the south and west. The incidence of such workers was especially high in the southwestern area, called the "Southern Commercial Area." It included Chersons, Tavrida, Kiev, Podolsk, and Bessarabia provinces. As a major Black Sea port, Odessa was central to the economic life of this area.

As shown in Map 2.6, this study uses workers in secondary industry per thousand population as the explanatory variable to indicate the level of industrial modernization of provinces. The entire worker-servant category is too broad to be used as an industrial variable. Also, use of the entire worker-servant category as the industrial modernization variable would compel the analysis to show that persons who held worker-servant jobs tended to live in areas with a high degree of industrial development. Secondary industrial worker jobs comprised less than half of all worker-servant jobs. Thus some degree of circularity is avoided. Also, the association of modern production methods with secondary industry has a theoretically satisfying relationship to Levy's industrially oriented definition of modernization.

Unfortunately, workers in secondary industry per thousand population refers to 1897 rather than to some earlier date. Some data were located on workers in industry per thousand population for earlier dates (as shown in Figure 2.3), but this covered a broader range of types of work than was desired. Also, the earlier data were not available separately for all provinces but rather individually for the provinces (usually twenty-five) with the largest absolute number of workers along with a total for all other provinces combined (Rashin 1940: 41, 162). Hopefully workers in secondary industry per thousand population for 1897 is highly correlated with workers in secondary industry for some earlier date, such as 1885. It is likely that this is true. The correlation with workers in industry per thousand population for 1860 is .803 on forty-one provinces and .860 on the twenty out of those forty-one provinces for which the number of workers is separately available. For the analysis of migration to St. Petersburg City in 1869, it would not be appropriate to use the percentage of the population engaged in secondary industry in 1897, since 1897 was almost thirty years after 1869. Explanatory variables should precede, or at least not follow in time, dependent variables. Thus for the analysis of migration in 1869, the number of workers in industry per thousand population in 1860 is used as the indicator of the level of industrial modernization of provinces of origin.

WORKER-SERVANT JOBS AND ORIGINS OF WORKER-SERVANTS

The extent to which the geographical distribution of worker-servant jobs predetermined the pattern of migration of those who held worker-servant jobs is relevant to this study. If, as this study argues, factors other than economic necessity affected migration decisions, then the amount of movement of persons for wage labor should be more than would be minimally necessary in order that the worker-servant positions in 1897 be filled. This section briefly investigates the extent to which the location of worker-servant jobs in 1897 predetermined the pattern of migration of those who became worker-servants. Although the evidence is presented for males, quite similar patterns appeared for females. The number of worker-servant jobs available and the number of worker-servant jobs available per thousand population differed greatly among provinces. Some provinces had many more such jobs in 1897 than there were natives of the province engaged in wage work. For other provinces, the only way a substantial proportion of the native population of the province could obtain wage work jobs would have been to migrate out of the province of birth.

Map 2.7 shows the extent to which natives of a province predominated in worker-servant jobs. The number of worker-servant jobs held by male natives of a province per thousand worker-servant jobs in the province is shown. The proportion of jobs held by natives is low in Moscow, St. Petersburg, and in parts of the Urals as well as in part of the

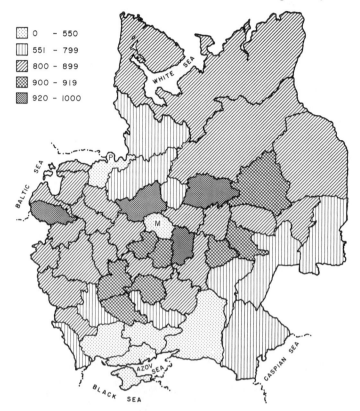

MAP 2.7   Native Male Workers Per Thousand Male Workers Resident
in Province: 1897

Southern Commercial Area. It is not surprising that the proportion of such jobs held by natives would be small where
there were so many worker-servant jobs available that they
could not all be filled by natives. If a large proportion of
migrants held worker-servant jobs simply because there
were many such jobs available, then areas with a high proportion of migrants in worker-servant jobs should also be
provinces where a large proportion of the native population

held worker-servant jobs. Map 2.8 shows the number of native male worker-servants per thousand native males living in the province. Natives were heavily involved in worker-servant jobs in and around Moscow and St. Petersburg and in some parts of the Urals. However, in the Donbass and in the Southern Commercial Area, a smaller proportion of native males held worker-servant jobs. This could have been either because in some areas migrants were more qualified than natives for available jobs or because persons in various

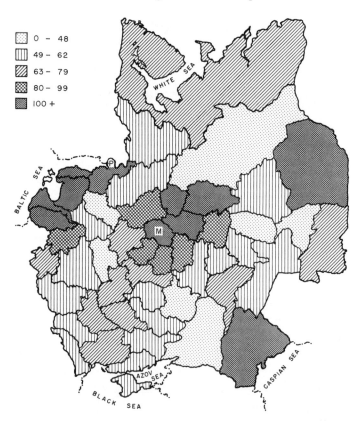

▨	0 – 48
⦀	49 – 62
▨	63 – 79
▨	80 – 99
■	100 +

MAP 2.8   Native Male Workers Per Thousand Native Males: 1897

areas differed in their desire to obtain wage work. This may imply that living in an area with a high degree of commercial activity is not necessarily a very modernizing experience.

To approach the question of the distribution of those in worker-servant jobs slightly differently, if the preceding argument is valid, then the variables shown in Maps 2.7 and 2.8 should be strongly negatively correlated. This is because the preceding argument contends that if a province has a large number of worker-servant jobs available, then although natives will take advantage of the job opportunities (resulting in high values for the variable shown in Map 2.8), migrants will also be so strongly attracted to the given province that the actual proportion of all worker-servants who are native to the province will be small (leading to low values of the variable shown in Map 2.7). In fact, on all fifty provinces, the correlation is only $-.049$. If the three Baltic provinces and Moscow and St. Petersburg provinces are excluded, the correlation is $.169$. Thus it seems that the migration pattern of those who in 1897 held worker-servant jobs was not totally determined by the geographic incidence of such jobs.

Given the distribution of worker jobs in 1897, the question of the extent to which worker migration was more than was necessary can be approached yet another way. One can imagine that certain persons were (hypothetically) destined to hold worker jobs in 1897. Such persons are identified as those who do hold worker jobs in 1897. The number of such persons generated by province A is the number of persons born in province A who in 1897 held wage work positions anywhere in the Russian Empire in 1897. This may be considered the demand for wage work positions in province A. The supply of wage work positions in province A is indicated by the number of wage work positions in province A in 1897. The difference between the number of natives of province A who in 1897 held wage work positions anywhere in the Russian Empire in 1897 and the number of wage work positions in province A in 1897 yields the minimal number of natives of province A who would have to migrate out of the province in order to hold wage work positions in 1897 if this difference is positive. If this difference is negative, then there were surplus wage work positions in the province, and it would not be necessary for any natives to move out. The sum of the positive differences is the amount of out-migration from provinces of birth necessary given the distribution of wage work positions in 1897. The actual migration of those who became wage workers is found by the difference between the number of natives of the province who in 1897 held wage work positions anywhere in the Russian Empire in 1897 and the number of natives of the province who in 1897 held wage work jobs but still lived in the province of birth. This is the actual out-migration of those who were born in the province and in 1897 were wage workers. The ratio of the actual worker out-migration (in the preceding terms) to the necessary worker out-migration gives a measure of the extent to which there was more migratory movement of those who became wage workers than was necessary given the distribution of wage work positions and given the persons who in 1897 held wage work jobs. For males this ratio is 1.5 and for females it is 1.6. Thus for each sex, there was over 50 percent more interprovincial migratory movement of those who ended up in wage work positions in 1897 than would be necessary in a mechanical sense. It is interesting that females were as likely as males (slightly more likely, in fact) to cross interprovincial boundaries to find wage work given the availability of female wage work positions in a province.

DESTINATIONS OF MIGRANTS

The majority of this study deals with lifetime migration as assessed by a cross-tabulation of province of birth by province (or city) of residence in 1897. The research includes only those persons who lived in the Russian Empire. Persons who died before 1897 and those who emigrated from the Russian Empire before 1897 are not considered. Such exclusions are not likely to affect the results.[9]

The study considers only those born in European Russia. Except for the analysis of all those who migrated out of their European Russian province of birth to anywhere in the Russian Empire, specific destinations are only considered in European Russia, Siberia, and Central Asia. Table 2.6 shows the distribution by sex of all persons born in the fifty provinces of European Russia who in 1897 were recorded as living in the Russian Empire. Over 84 percent of the outmigrants of each sex lived in European Russia, Siberia, or Central Asia in this year. Most migrants lived in European

[9] It is unlikely that the exclusion of persons who died before 1897 has a substantial effect on the results, as medical evidence indicates that a person's mortality experience is generally similar to the mortality experience of the area in which he spent the first fifteen years of his life (Burch 1962). Thus, if the death rates of migrants from an area and those who remained in an area were the same, then migration rates would be unaffected.

The mass of emigration from the Russian Empire did not begin until after 1900 and consisted largely of Jews from the western provinces. Thus it is unlikely for migration as assessed in 1897 that emigration played a major role. Period migration to Siberia and Central Asia after 1900 did occur at a time when emigration was heavy. However, Jews were rarely migrants to Siberia or Central Asia. Even in provinces where Jews were a relatively large proportion of the population, they still were rarely more than 10 percent even in 1897. Thus, it is unlikely that the conclusions about migration to Siberia and Central Asia up to 1909 would be seriously affected by international emigration.

TABLE 2.6

DISTRIBUTION OF PERSONS BORN IN EUROPEAN RUSSIA
BY RESIDENCE IN 1897

		Male	Female
I.	Persons born in European Russia in thousands	47,027	48,470
II.	Persons living in the Russian Empire not in their province of birth, of those born in European Russia in thousands	5,516	3,880
	% of persons born in European Russia living in the Russian Empire not in their province of birth	11.7%	8.0%

% Distribution of Persons Born in European Russia Living in the Russian Empire Not in Their Province of Birth (% distribution of II)		
In European Russia not in province of birth	69.3	72.1
In Siberia	11.2	11.8
In Central Asia	3.5	3.5
In Caucasus	10.4	11.2
In Russian Poland	5.2	1.4
In Finland, Bukhara, Khiva or other encampments	.5	.1
Total	100.1%	100.1%

NOTE: Total does not add to 100.0% due to rounding error.

Russia. The research considers Siberia and Central Asia as destinations because they seemed good examples of agricultural frontier destinations. Substantial free migration to both destinations began only shortly before 1897. The study does not consider the Caucasus as a separate destination because detailed data of the type available for Siberia and Central Asia were not readily available. The research also excludes Russian Poland because much migration there was compulsory military migration. Over five times as many males as females were lifetime migrants from European Russia to Russian Poland in 1897. Some analysis was performed with Russian Polish destinations included with general European Russian destinations, but this had little effect on the results. For every province for each sex, migration to the parts of the Russian Empire studied as detailed destinations was more important than migration to those parts of the Russian Empire not considered in detail. In every case the volume of migration out of the province of birth to another province in European Russia, Siberia, or Central Asia was greater than the volume of such migration to provinces in the Caucasus, Russian Poland, or the encampments.

Maps 2.9 and 2.10 show the distribution of male and

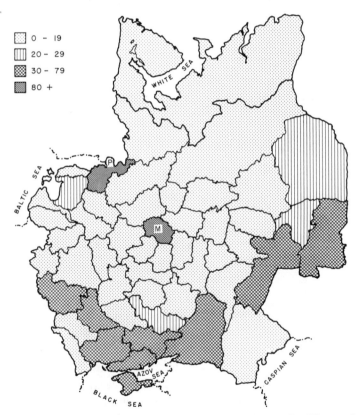

MAP 2.9   Male In-Migrants by Province of Destination Per Thousand Male In-Migrants to European Russia: 1897

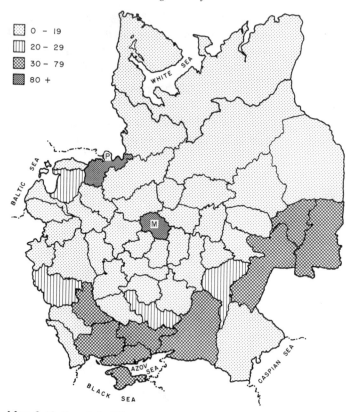

MAP 2.10 Female In-Migrants by Province of Destination Per Thousand Female In-Migrants to European Russia: 1897

female interprovincial migrants born in the Russian Empire who lived in European Russia in 1897 (the values for Moscow and St. Petersburg are for the provinces). Moscow, St. Petersburg, the Urals, the Donbass, and the Southern Commercial Area were areas of heavy in-migration. The research studies Moscow and St. Petersburg cities, the Urals (Perm and Orenburg provinces), the Donbass (Don and Ekaterinoslav provinces), and the rest of European Russia combined separately in some detail as destinations within European Russia.

This study considers Moscow and St. Petersburg cities as modern urban destinations and Siberia and Central Asia as agricultural frontiers. The Urals and Donbass are mining areas where free agricultural land was more recently available than it was for most of the rest of European Russia. These areas of mining and recent agricultural settlement are seen as intermediate in industrial modernization between Moscow and St. Petersburg cities and Asiatic Russia. The distribution of migrants by destination within European Russia is shown in Table 2.7.

Table 2.8 shows the distribution of worker-servants by

TABLE 2.7

DISTRIBUTION OF MIGRANTS BY DESTINATION WITHIN
EUROPEAN RUSSIA: 1897

	Male	Female
Number born in European Russia	47,026,568	48,470,223
Number living in European Russia not in province of birth	3,821,925	2,795,633
% Outmigrants within European Russia	8.1%	5.8%
% Distribution of Outmigrants within European Russia		
Moscow City	7.7	6.2
St. Petersburg City	11.4	10.1
Don Basin (Don and Ekat)	10.4	10.3
Urals (Perm and Oren)	5.5	6.7
Kiev City	1.7	1.6
Odessa	2.5	2.4
Elsewhere in European Russia	60.8	62.7
Total	100.0%	100.0%

TABLE 2.8

DISTRIBUTION OF WORKERS AND SERVANTS WITHIN DESTINATIONS
OF INTEREST: 1897

	Male				Female			
	M-St.P	E-MSDU	D-U	AsRus	M-St.P	E-MSDU	D-U	AsRus
Pop in Thou	1,285	44,003	4,620	7,108	1,019	43,022	4,652	6,358
Pop W+S in Thou	591	3,482	536	553	276	1,757	167	114
%W+S	46.0	7.9	11.6	7.8	27.1	4.2	3.6	1.8

% Distribution of Workers and Servants

*Sec Ind	54.6	34.0	26.2	13.9	28.6	13.4	6.4	2.8
*Metal	.1	.7	20.8	5.9	0	.1	4.7	.4
Rural Ec	1.0	32.8	25.2	41.7	.2	29.6	20.2	30.2
Unskilled	7.1	11.1	9.7	24.6	5.4	10.1	2.8	1.4
%TC+C	21.0	8.3	9.6	6.2	4.6	1.8	2.8	1.4
*Fact Serv	1.0	4.0	2.8	.5	.1	.8	.5	.1
*Adm+Soc Serv	3.8	2.4	1.6	1.6	3.4	.7	.7	.6
HHServ	11.1	6.5	5.1	5.6	57.7	48.5	56.7	50.3
Total	99.7%	100.0%	100.0%	100.0%	100.0%	100.0%	100.0%	99.9%

Without Rural Economy

Pop W+S in Thou	585	2,349	401	322	275	1,237	188	77
% W+S	45.6	5.3	8.7	4.5	27.0	2.9	2.9	1.2

% Distribution of Workers and Servants

*Sec Ind	55.2	50.6	35.0	23.8	28.7	19.0	8.0	4.0
*Metal	.1	1.0	27.8	10.1	0	.1	5.9	.6
Unskilled	7.2	16.5	13.0	42.2	.2	14.3	10.2	20.2
*TC&C	21.2	12.6	11.5	10.6	5.4	2.6	3.5	2.0
*Fact Serv	1.0	6.0	3.7	.9	4.6	1.1	.6	.1
*Adm+Soc Serv	3.8	3.6	2.1	2.7	3.4	1.0	.9	.9
HH Serv	11.2	9.7	6.8	9.6	57.8	61.8	71.1	72.1
Total	99.7%	100.0%	99.9%	99.9%	100.1%	99.9%	100.2%	99.9%
%rel mod inc rur	80.5	49.6	60.0	28.1	36.4	16.8	15.1	5.3
%rel mod exc rur	81.8	73.8	80.1	48.1	42.1	23.8	18.9	7.6

NOTE: * indicates relatively modern occupations, TC&C represents transportation, communication and commerce.

sex within each of these destinations of detailed interest.
The impact of mining on the labor force distribution is clear
in the Urals-Don area. It is apparent that Moscow and St.
Petersburg have the most modern occupational distributions
for each sex (more secondary industry and more commer-

cial activity), while Asiatic Russia has the least modern occupational distribution. As noted earlier, workers in the rural economy are included in the worker-servant classification. The bottom panel of Table 2.8 considers the occupational distribution after excluding workers in the rural economy. This adjustment shows clearly that for nonagricultural activity, females in Moscow or St. Petersburg cities are less likely to be engaged in domestic service than are females in other destinations. Although males everywhere are less frequently engaged in domestic service than females, the pattern of lesser involvement in domestic service in the two great cities does not hold for males.

Adjusting for activity in the rural economy also leaves the smallest proportion of each sex in unskilled and day laborer jobs in the two great cities. When the job categories are classified as relatively modern or relatively traditional, the Don and Urals areas appear more modern for males than other areas (excluding Moscow or St. Petersburg cities) in European Russia, while the opposite is true for females. For both sexes, the great cities are the most modern, and Asiatic Russia is the least modern.

Moscow and St. Petersburg had the highest literacy levels for each sex of all specific destinations considered, while Asiatic Russia had the lowest literacy levels. The Don and Urals mining areas did not differ substantially in literacy from the rest of European Russia.

Kiev and Odessa are considered as candidates for modern destinations for Jews and for others from areas of heavy Jewish settlement. Thus the provinces in which Kiev and Odessa are located are excluded only for that subanalysis. The rest of the analysis excludes the six provinces in which the major destinations in European Russia are located as well as the three Baltic provinces, in order to have a comparable universe for comparisons.

RELATIONS AMONG EXPLANATORY VARIABLES

Table 2.9 shows the mean and the standard deviation of each of the major explanatory variables used in this study, except for the various distance measures. Table 2.10 shows the intercorrelations among the explanatory variables. These tables should be useful references throughout the study. As indicated earlier in this chapter, areas high in literacy tend to be high in the level of industrial moderniza-

TABLE 2.9

MEANS, STANDARD DEVIATIONS AND DEFINITIONS OF VARIOUS
EXPLANATORY VARIABLES

Name	Definition	Mean	s.d.
Soil	Soil fertility level 1-5, 1=lowest, 5=highest	3.293	1.470
Agri w/aux	Number of males whose primary occupation was in agriculture who had an auxiliary occupation per thousand males whose primary occupation was in agriculture 1897	235.796	122.240
Lit7483	Percent of military recruits who were literate 1874-1883	22.293	11.007
Lit94	Percent of military recruits who were literate 1894	40.073	14.742
Lit04	Percent of military recruits who were literate 1904	58.415	14.620
Work60	Number of workers in industry per thousand population 1860	7.927	10.801
WorkSec97	Number of workers in secondary industry per thousand population 1897	16.179	14.691
Nat r6165	Natural rate of increase 1861-1865	14.268	3.969
Nat r8185	Natural rate of increase 1881-1885	13.561	3.479
Nat r8690	Natural rate of increase 1886-1890	15.171	3.130
Nat r9195	Natural rate of increase 1891-1895	12.683	4.714
Nat r9600	Natural rate of increase 1896-1900	16.659	2.972
Nat r0105	Natural rate of increase 1901-1905	15.854	3.038
GR8597	Growth rate 1885-1897 per thousand	10.056	8.417
Density97	Hundreds of persons per square mile 1897	1.831	.892

(Continued, p. 68)

TABLE 2.10

CORRELATIONS AMONG EXPLANATORY VARIABLES (ON 41 PROVINCES)

	Soil	Agri w/aux	Lit7483	Lit94	Lit04	WorkSec97	Work60	Nat r6165	Nat r8185	Nat r8690	Nat r9195	Nat r9600	Nat r0105	GR8597	Density 97
Soil	1.000														
Agri w/aux	-.554	1.000													
Lit7483	-.609	.641	1.000												
Lit94	-.503	.683	.944	1.000											
Lit04	-.473	.594	.832	.920	1.000										
WorkSec97	-.261	.457	.678	.674	.605	1.000									
Work60	-.060	.264	.267	.301	.279	.803	1.000								
Nat r6165	.308	-.663	-.460	-.456	-.349	-.283	-.163	1.000							
Nat r8185	.363	-.517	-.629	-.607	-.511	-.420	-.168	.527	1.000						
Nat r8690	.402	-.604	-.676	-.683	-.591	-.466	-.233	.620	.746	1.000					
Nat r9195	-.156	-.256	-.199	-.225	-.184	-.100	-.092	.555	.479	.529	1.000				
Nat r9600	.584	.585	-.626	-.577	-.447	-.354	-.163	.610	.815	.773	.438	1.000			
Nat r0105	.732	.483	-.595	-.518	-.417	-.238	.005	.468	.630	.642	.119	.847	1.000		
GR8597	-.102	-.353	-.325	-.423	-.402	-.222	-.126	.469	.614	.670	.780	.521	.521	1.000	
Density 97	.658	-.486	-.373	-.306	-.271	-.043	.089	.388	.182	.332	.115	.327	.327	.022	1.000

TABLE 2.10 (continued)

	ln Dist M-St.P	ln Dist St.P	ln Dist M	% Closer St.P than M	ln Dist Asia. Russia	ln Dist. U-D	ln Dist Urals	ln Dist Donbass	% Closer D than U
Soil	.377	.661	.178	-.377	-.171	-.569	-.096	-.562	-.511
Agr w/aux	-.465	-.382	-.365	.465	-.151	.306	-.264	.251	-.231
Lit7484	-.568	-.406	-.560	.568	.033	.292	-.070	.168	-.168
Lit94	-.678	-.410	-.684	.678	-.026	.125	-.134	.033	.056
Lit04	-.677	-.364	-.696	.677	-.023	-.018	-.151	-.112	.075
WorkSec97	-.442	-.104	-.545	-.395	-.051	-.048	-.092	.000	-.035
Work60	-.277	.029	-.365	-.353	-.117	-.245	-.124	-.066	.029
Nat r6165	.364	.324	.233	-.364	.383	-.064	.432	-.206	.176
Nat r8185	.585	.469	.499	-.585	-.010	-.271	.036	-.066	.050
Nat r8690	.488	.298	.447	-.488	.291	-.151	.356	-.073	.049
Nat r9195	.284	-.036	.262	-.284	.547	.193	.559	.213	-.216
Nat r9600	.577	.601	.399	-.557	.065	-.424	.096	-.413	.393
Nat r0105	.490	.730	.267	-.490	-.207	-.594	-.176	-.558	.518
GR8597	.532	.096	.578	.441	.406	.210	.442	.372	.518
Density 97	.052	.262	-.121	-.347	.389	-.259	.456	-.428	.364

NOTE: $p < .05$ for underlined coefficients, two-tailed tests

tion. Also, provinces in which traditional agriculture is quite important tend to be low in literacy and somewhat low in the level of industrial modernization. Areas where traditional agriculture is important tend to have high levels of natural increase, while areas with high literacy levels or a large proportion of the population in secondary industry tend to have fairly low levels of natural increase. All of these relations are reasonable and are typical of a modernizing society.

CHAPTER 3

Out-Migration from the Province of Birth

Examination of out-migration can yield some insight into the changing nature of European Russian society as well as provide the general background against which migration to more specific destinations can be considered. Since the set of possible destinations is very diverse, and since provinces will differ in the proportion of out-migrants who choose various destinations, the explanation of general out-migration is not expected to be as clear as may be the case for migration to more specific destinations. However, examination of general out-migration can indicate whether the model proposed is generally correct.

This chapter considers migration out of a European Russian province of birth, regardless of the destination, as long as the out-migrant lived in the Russian Empire in 1897. The measure used to study general out-migration is a rate that for province A has as numerator the number of persons born in province A who in 1897 did not live in province A but still lived in the Russian Empire. It has as denominator the number of persons in thousands born in province A who in 1897 lived anywhere in the Russian Empire, including those living in province A. Neither numerator nor denominator consider persons who died before 1897 nor those who migrated out of the Russian Empire before that year.[1]

---

[1] See Chapter 2 for a discussion of the possible effects of exclusion of those who died or were international emigrants. The period of time to which a lifetime migration rate refers depends on the age of persons. Aside from the problems of international emigration and possible differential mortality according to migration statue, this rate is proper since the denominator is the proper population at risk of being lifetime migrants—

Even if a person were born in Bessarabia and lived in Bessarabia in 1897, he might not have spent his entire life in Bessarabia. He could have been born in Bessarabia in 1850, migrated to Kiev in 1865, and migrated back to Bessarabia in 1896. In 1897 he would be counted as living in his province of birth and for the purposes of this study would not be considered a migrant. Elderly persons returning to retire in the province in which they grew up would provide examples of such behavior. Such return migration may also have been common for those who migrated to an urban or industrial area in order to obtain wage work and then returned to their place of birth either after having accumulated sufficient savings or after they became discouraged with the work they were doing in a factory or other establishment.

A concern of studies of migrants resident at a destination is the extent to which those migrants who remain in industrial or urban centers represent only a select portion of the migrants to the given destination. The selectivity process might favor those who were more successful, with the less successful migrants returning home (Kuznets 1964; Sanders 1969). Although the data examined do not indicate the extent of return migration, there is reason to believe that the effect of such migration on the general pattern of the data may not be great. Although seasonal migration was common in many areas (Johnson 1976), since the census was taken in January, it would be likely that those who were seasonally working in urban or industrial areas away from their homes would have been at such seasonal employment when the census was taken.

Return migration due to discouragement also occurred for

---

that is, those persons born in province A, regardless of where they lived, are the population who are candidates for being lifetime migrants from province of birth, A.

migration to Asiatic Russia. In the chapter on Asiatic Russia, data are examined that imply that the pattern of gross migration (those who migrated to a given destination whether or not they stayed there) was very strongly related to the pattern of net migration (the gross migration, less those who were return migrants from Asiatic Russia to European Russia). Thus it is likely that the general out-migration rate is a reasonable indicator of the rate of migration out of a province without returning within some specified time.

Out-migration as detected from a cross-classification of province of birth by province of residence does not detect movement within a province. This exclusion of intraprovincial migration presents some problems, since provinces differ in size and shape. Generally, this study considers a migration to be a move that covers a certain minimal distance, although this minimal distance differs among provinces and according to centrality of the place of birth in a province. The problem of detecting migration within a province is only serious when the destination considered is a major city. Migration from the hinterland of Moscow province to Moscow City seemed such a major move that it should not be considered as movement within the same province. Since it is not generally possible to detect whether the place of birth was in the city or in the hinterland of the province, Moscow and St. Petersburg provinces were excluded from consideration as places of birth.[2]

The proposed model of migration leads to the expectation that out-migration will be positively related to the literacy

[2] Although the detailed provincial volumes (Russia 1899-1904) would allow this distinction to be made for the total population by sex, it was not possible for those engaged in wage work. Thus, in order to have a comparable set of origins, these provinces were excluded from the set of origins considered.

rate in the province of birth. Underlying this prediction is the hypothesis that areas with relatively high rates of literacy will tend to produce more persons willing to assume the risks associated with migration than will places with lower levels of literacy. The model also predicts that places with a high proportion of the population working in secondary industry will have high out-migration rates because these areas generate in their residents a propensity to view industrial work and other non-agricultural opportunities favorably. On the other hand, it is expected that heavy involvement in traditional agriculture (indicated by a high level of soil fertility) tends to make persons less willing to undertake risks of any type, including those associated with migration. However, the degree of influence of these two types of factors is expected to vary according to the nature of the destination. The positive effect of the level of industrial development of the origin is expected to be stronger if the destination is an industrial center rather than an agricultural frontier, while a high level of soil fertility is expected to be less of an impediment to migration to an agricultural frontier than to an industrial center. Contrary to the arguments of many other researchers, this study does not expect that natural r will be strongly positively related to out-migration. Instead, it holds that objective factors, such as population pressure, are not generally the most important factors in migration. Only under special conditions are factors such as population pressure expected to be important. Such conditions are examined in the chapter on Asiatic Russia.

Table 3.1 shows the correlations between the explanatory variables and the migration rates and among the migration rates. The correlations that are statistically significant at the 5 percent level are underlined. "Statistical significance" at the 5 percent level (alternatively termed $p < .05$) means that correlations as large in absolute value would be obtained by

TABLE 3.1

CORRELATIONS FOR GENERAL OUT-MIGRATION: 1897 (ON 41 PROVINCES)

	M	F	MW	FW	MNW	FNW
Soil	.012	.187	-.194	-.234	.246	.374
Lit7483	.514	.261	.379	.382	.332	.087
WorkSec97	.415	.165	.071	.028	.379	.101
Nat r8135	-.481	-.281	-.497	-.441	-.334	-.147
M	1.000	.859	.733	.656	.929	.774
F		1.000	.645	.660	.867	.961
MW			1.000	.890	.525	.490
FW				1.000	.427	.471
MNW					1.000	.877
FNW						1.000
Mean	121.419	79.866	366.799	280.590	91.933	70.358
s.d.	45.886	27.097	140.254	129.727	29.933	23.975

NOTE: $p < .05$ for underlined coefficients, two-tailed tests.

pure chance, rather than due to a true linear relationship, only 5 percent of the time. All of the statistically significant correlations between explanatory variables and migration rates are in the expected direction except for the correlation between soil fertility and the female non-worker out-migration rate.

Migration rates are generally high out of more literate provinces and out of those provinces with a low rate of natural increase. The negative relationship of natural r with the migration rate for all groups except female non-workers counters the general importance of population pressure stressed in much of the literature. It also counters specific speculation about population pressure as a general cause of out-migration in late nineteenth-century European Russia (Leasure and Lewis 1968; Robinson 1969). The statistically significant positive coefficients for secondary industry for males generally and for male non-workers specifically give some support for the expectation that out-migration rates would be positively related to the level of industrial modernization of the origin.

The pattern of correlations differs according to work status in 1897. The positive relationship with literacy is stronger for workers than for non-workers. Also the correlations with soil fertility are negative for workers and positive for non-workers. This pattern of literacy is consistent with the supposition that those who desired wage work jobs but lived in highly literate provinces were more likely to be willing to leave their birth province in order to find such jobs than were those who desired wage work jobs but lived in less literate provinces. Recall from Chapter 2 that there was 50 percent more movement of wage workers across provincial boundaries than would have been necessary to match the distribution of wage work jobs with the distribution by place of birth of those who became wage workers in 1897.

The difference in the relation of soil fertility to out-migration rates by work status is related to the different types of destinations that workers tended to choose as compared to non-workers. As will be seen later, those who engaged in wage work in 1897 were somewhat more likely to have migrated to major urban centers than those who did not engage in wage work during the same year. Non-workers in 1897 consisted of two very different types of persons. For migrants to major urban destinations, such as Moscow or St. Petersburg, non-workers were generally either children or wives without wage work jobs. However, the census categories also define as non-workers those engaged only in subsistence agriculture. As the vast majority of migrants living in Asiatic Russia in 1897 were subsistence farmers, the bulk of migration to Asiatic Russia consisted of those who were not wage workers in 1897. Comparisons across various destinations of workers in 1897 are thus more valid than comparisons across various destinations of non-workers in 1897 because the former group is more homogeneous. However, even when a specific destination is considered, differences are quite generally found in the pattern of origins of workers as compared to non-worker migrants to that destination.

Maps 3.1 and 3.2 show the out-migration rates for female workers and female non-workers. Female worker out-migration was fairly common near Moscow and St. Petersburg and in the more northerly area. The female non-worker rates are high in the central southern part of the high soil fertility area.

The patterns for males are quite similar to those for females by work status in 1897. This similarity is indicated by the high correlations between male and female worker migration rates and between male and female non-worker migration rates, as shown in the lower portion of Table 3.1. The high degree of relationship between male and female rates within the same work status is substantively interesting. Table 2.5 shows that male and female workers in 1897 were engaged in very different types of work. Recall that 46 percent of female workers in 1897 were domestic servants.

Most theories of nineteenth-century Russian peasant family structure referring to the period before the emancipation of the serfs in the 1860s describe the Russian peasant family as ruled by a patriarchal father, who closely supervised the activities of all family members. According to this theory, young women would have been very much subject to their father's control (Vucinich 1968; Pipes 1974: 16-17). After emancipation, the legal control of the father over family members was weakened, and one might suppose that his actual control was also reduced (Robinson 1969: 228). If the

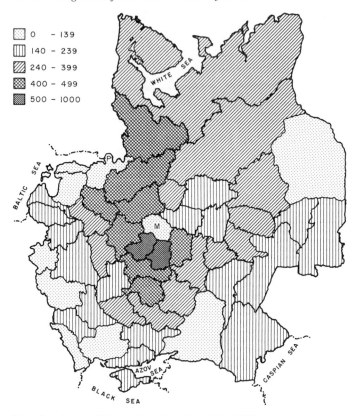

MAP 3.1 Female Worker Out-Migration Rate: 1897

father continued to exert substantial control over the activities of all family members after emancipation, one might suspect that a young woman who sought wage work before 1897, even as a household servant, would have been much less likely to have left her province of birth than a male seeking wage work. Instead, if the traditional view of the Russian peasant family was accurate for the pre-emancipation period and if it continued to be accurate for the remainder of the nineteenth century, she would be expected to

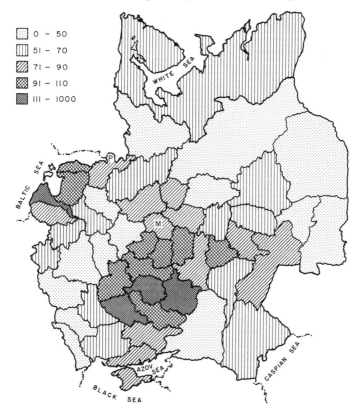

MAP 3.2 Female Non-Worker Out-Migration Rate: 1897

have sought a domestic service position in a provincial center rather than in a more distant location across provincial boundaries.

Theresa McBride (1976) found that during the industrial revolution female domestic servants in England and France tended to travel quite far in order to obtain wage work and often obtained such work through kin connections. Even though kin connections probably were important in obtaining domestic service jobs in nineteenth-century European

Russia, one might expect that a family would be as likely to have kin connections that could be utilized to obtain domestic service employment for a female family member in a provincial center as in a more distant location.

In Chapter 2, it was shown that given the distribution of wage work jobs in 1897, women who obtained wage work positions were as likely as men who obtained wage work positions to cross provincial boundaries, even if wage work positions suitable for the given sex were available in the province of birth. The mean out-migration rates at the bottom of Table 3.1 show that in European Russia, a woman who obtained wage work in 1897 (even if the distribution of such jobs is ignored) was 76 percent as likely to have left her province of birth before taking such a job as was a man who engaged in wage work in the same year. This was the case even though the seasonal migration for wage work referred to earlier was more typical of males than of females.

With some exceptions, a general finding throughout this study is that in 1897 the pattern of migration is more similar by work status than by sex. This finding suggests that women in late nineteenth-century European Russia may have exercised more independent decision-making power than has generally been supposed. They may have been responding to the same kinds of motivations and inducements for migration as men, even though the tasks performed by female wage workers were quite different from the tasks performed by male wage workers. This interpretation suggests that in a society at a fairly early stage of modernization, as was late nineteenth-century European Russia, when wage work is fairly uncommon, the fact of engaging in wage work may be more important than the specific content of the work. Lewis's (1954) distinction between modern and traditional jobs considers an important aspect of jobs in the modern sector to be the inclusion of a wage as opposed to the fulfillment of a personal family obligation without monetary reimbursement. Thus even though domestic servants were probably paid partly in room and board, some wages were also typically included, and as great as may have been the supervision of the employer's family over a domestic servant, it is likely that it was less than would have been the supervision of the servant's own family over her activities, especially if she were fairly young. Therefore even moving into domestic service may have been behavior that entailed a fair amount of risk to the individual.

The combined effects of the explanatory variables considered in Table 3.1 can also be examined. One method of examining the joint effect of a set of variables is through a multiple regression. In a multiple regression, a coefficient is assigned to each explanatory variable to indicate what its relationship with the dependent variable would be if its effect on that variable were assessed after *all* of the other explanatory variables had been related to it. For instance, if a multiple regression related the male out-migration rate (the dependent variable) to a literacy and a secondary industry variable (the explanatory variables), the coefficient of the literacy variable would reflect what literacy could explain about the variability in the male out-migration rate after the effect of secondary industry had been accounted for. Similarly, the coefficient of the secondary industry variable would represent the variability in the out-migration rate accounted for by the industrial variable after the effect of literacy had been taken into account. Because of this dependency of the explanatory variables, if two strongly related explanatory variables are entered together in the same multiple regression, then the magnitude of the measured effect of each on the dependent variable will be depressed. Table 2.10 clearly reveals that several of the explanatory variables are strongly correlated. This intercorrelation makes it unlikely that several of these correlated independent variables could be statistically significant in the same equation unless the underlying relationships between them and the dependent variable were exceedingly strong.

Table 3.2 shows the results of two different types of multiple regressions. Standardized multiple regression coefficients are shown. This standardization transforms the explanatory variables so that each has a mean of zero and a standard deviation of one, thus making unimportant differences in the units in which the various explanatory variables are measured. The interpretation of coefficients is essentially similar to that for correlation coefficients.[3] Stand-

[3] There is some disagreement in the literature concerning when standardized and when unstandardized multiple regression coefficients should be examined (Duncan 1975). Some writers contend that when comparisons of coefficients are made within equations, it is proper to examine standardized regression coefficients but that when comparisons are made of coefficients in different equations, the unstandardized coefficients should be examined. The relationship between the unstandardized and the standardized coefficients is determined by the standard deviation of the dependent variable and the independent variable to which the coefficient refers in the following manner:

$$\text{Stand}_{yx} = \text{Unstand}_{yx}(S_x/S_y)$$

where

Stand_{yx} = standardized multiple regression coefficient with dependent variable y and explanatory variable x

Unstand_{yx} = unstandardized multiple regression coefficient

S_x = standard deviation of x

S_y = standard deviation of y

Since the same variables are used throughout the analysis, the only source of difference between the standardized and unstandardized coefficients of a variable is the standard deviation of the dependent migration variable. It did not seem that this source of difference should influ-

ardized multiple regression coefficients generally range from −1 to +1. It is possible, although rare, for the coefficients to fall outside of the −1 to +1 range. If a correlation of a given absolute magnitude is statistically significantly different from zero at the 5 percent level (for instance a correlation of .351), then for the same number of cases in the analysis any correlation of greater absolute magnitude (for instance .352) will also be significantly different from zero at the 5 percent level. On the other hand, the relationship of statistical significance to the magnitude of coefficients is not as exact for standardized regression coefficients as it is for correlation coefficients. Although a multiple regression coefficient with a larger absolute value is more likely to be statistically significant than a coefficient with a smaller absolute value, exceptions to this tendency sometimes occur. Thus a (slightly) smaller standardized regression coefficient may 'be statistically significant while a (slightly) larger standardized regression coefficient is not significant even

---

ence the interpretation of the relationships found. When standardized regression coefficients are compared, one is comparing the relative effect rather than the absolute effect of explanatory variables on various dependent variables. Unstandardized coefficients are useful for policy-oriented or descriptive studies. For instance, if a researcher were studying the effect of education on income, with education measured in years of schooling and income measured in dollars, the unstandardized regression coefficient for education could be interpreted as the increment in dollars of income that is associated with an increment in education of one year. However, the primary purpose of this research is analytic rather than descriptive or policy-oriented. Thus the standardized coefficients seemed more appropriate to this study's purposes than the unstandardized coefficients. The interested reader can compute any desired unstandardized regression coefficient using the above formula, the standard deviations of the explanatory variables given in Table 2.9, and the standard deviations of the migration variables given in the relevant chapter in the table containing correlations between explanatory variables and migration rates.

TABLE 3.2

STEPWISE AND NON-STEPWISE STANDARDIZED MULTIPLE REGRESSIONS FOR
GENERAL OUT-MIGRATION (ON 41 PROVINCES)

	M	F	MW	FW	MNW	FNW
Stepwise Regressions						
Soil	.516	.333			.370	.679
	(11.20)	(4.44)			(6.65)	(15.69)
Lit7483	.643					.501
	(28.83)					(8.55)
WorkSec97					.475	
					(10.97)	
Nat r8185		-.402	-.497	-.441		
		(6.46)	(12.78)	(9.39)		
R^2	.431	.175	.247	.194	.271	.298
F	14.42	4.04	12.78	9.39	7.06	8.05
Non-Stepwise Regressions						
Soil	.513	.591	.138	.097	.684	.704
	(8.60)	(10.43)	(.59)	(.29)	(18.05)	(15.24)
Lit7483	.685	.641	.457	.543	.569	.518
	(6.60)	(5.69)	(3.03)	(4.20)	(5.80)	(3.82)
WorkSec97	-.018	-.187	-.379	-.451	.093	-.120
	(.01)	(.90)	(3.87)	(5.36)	(.29)	(.38)
Nat r8185	-.244	-.171	-.418	-.323	-.184	-.127
	(2.43)	(.90)	(5.66)	(3.31)	(1.35)	(.51)
R^2	.468	.295	.328	.314	.454	.315
F	7.91	3.77	4.39	4.13	7.48	4.14

NOTE: $p < .05$ for underlined coefficients. F ratios in parentheses.

when the number of units of analysis and the number of explanatory variables in the analysis remain unchanged.

The statistical significance of a regression coefficient is determined by examining the ratio of two quantities. The numerator equals the amount of variation in the dependent variable accounted for by the variation in the explanatory variable after the effects of the other explanatory variables in the analysis have been accounted for. The denominator equals the remaining unexplained variability in the dependent variable, adjusted by the number of cases in the analysis and the number of explanatory variables in the equation. This ratio, called the F ratio, indicates the significance of either individual regression coefficients or entire regression equations. The larger the F ratio, the more likely the coefficient (or equation) is to explain a significant amount of the variability in the dependent variable. The actual significance of the F ratio does depend on the number of explanatory variables in the equation and the number of cases in the analysis. In the tables presenting multiple regression results, F values for coefficients and for equations are presented, and the significance of such are indicated.

The top half of Table 3.2 shows the results of a stepwise multiple regression. The explanatory variable that explained the greatest amount of variability in the dependent variable was entered first. The variable that in combination with the first variable entered explained the greatest amount of variability in the dependent variable was entered next. This process continued as long as every variable included at a given point individually made a significant contribution to the explanation of the variability in the dependent variable at the 5 percent level. The R^2 value shows the proportion of the variance in the dependent variable that is jointly accounted for by the explanatory variables in the equation. Thus all of the coefficients for the explanatory variables at the top of Table 3.2 are statistically significantly different from zero at the 5 percent level, and all of the equations as a whole explain a significant amount of the variability in the dependent variable under consideration.

The results of the stepwise regressions suggest that soil fertility was more important than was implied in the correlations. The relationship of soil fertility to the out-migration rates is positive and significant for all groups except wage workers. As in the correlations, the patterns for workers are quite different from those for non-workers.

The lower part of Table 3.2 shows the results of multiple regressions in which all of the explanatory variables were entered simultaneously. Significant coefficients at the 5 percent level are indicated by underlining. When the equation as a whole explains a significant amount of the variability in the dependent variable, the R^2 value for the equation is underlined. All of the equations, except for the female group as a whole, explain a significant amount of the variability in the dependent variables.

Interpretation of individual coefficients in an equation that as a whole does not explain a significant amount of the variability in the dependent variable must be done cautiously. Even though the non-stepwise regression for females was insignificant, this does not mean that none of the explanatory variables were significantly related to female out-migration. In the stepwise regression, soil fertility and natural r were statistically significant, and the equation as a whole was significant. In a multiple regression, the significance of the F ratio for the equation depends on the number of explanatory variables in the regression equation, among other factors. The greater the number of explanatory variables, the higher the F ratio for the equation must be in order for the equation as a whole to be statistically significant. Thus, even if some explanatory variables are significantly related to the dependent variable, the addition of variables to the analysis that do not contribute further to the explanation of the variability in the dependent variable may cause the entire equation to lose its statistical significance. However, if one wishes to compare the joint effects of a set of variables in two different cases, the same explanatory variables must be entered in both analyses.

The non-stepwise regression results imply that for each sex considered as a whole, the most important factors related to out-migration rates were the soil fertility of the origin and the literacy level at the origin, both working positively, even though soil fertility was not significant in the correlations for total sex groups. One way to interpret this is that if the level of literacy of a province is held constant, then a higher level of soil fertility in a province leads to a higher level of out-migration. The correlation coefficients of soil fertility with most out-migration rates were insignificant because literacy is overall negatively related to soil fertility (correlation of $-.609$). Thus, in general, the higher the soil fertility, the lower the literacy. Literacy's strong positive effect on out-migration usually made this variable statistically significant both in the correlations and the regressions. These results suggest that explicit cultural modernization can overcome whatever conservative influence traditional agricultural may exert on willingness to migrate.

Even within the higher soil fertility area, out-migrants disproportionately came from the more literate provinces. Within the group of provinces at soil fertility levels 3-5, the correlation between the literacy variable and the male group as a whole was .493, and with male non-workers it was .370.

The change in the sign of soil fertility for several groups when literacy was included in an equation with soil fertility suggested another approach to the analysis of the joint effects of soil fertility and literacy on the propensity of persons to migrate out of their province of birth. A variable can be created that detects whether the effect of two variables together is greater than their separate additive effects. This is an interaction term. The interaction variable investigated in this analysis was created by the product of the literacy variable and the soil fertility variable. Considering forty-one provinces, this interaction variable was significantly positive for sex groups as a whole and for non-workers of each sex. This means that if a province was simultaneously high in soil fertility and in literacy, this was related to a high out-migration rate from that province for all groups except those who engaged in wage work in 1897. Correlations with this interaction variable and the stepwise regression results, including the interaction term, are shown in Table 3.3. The amount of variability explained by the interaction variable alone is comparable to the amount explained when the soil

TABLE 3.3

RELATIONS OF GENERAL OUT-MIGRATION RATES TO SOIL FERTILITY-
LITERACY INTERACTION (ON 41 PROVINCES)

	M	F	MW	FW	MNW	FNW
Correlations Soil Fertility- Literacy Interact	.573	.525	.170	.155	.648	.557

Standardized Stepwise Regression Coefficients

	M	F	MW	FW	MNW	FNW
Nat r8185	-.358 (6.22)		-.500 (12.78)	-.441 (9.39)		
Soil Fertility- Literacy Inter act	.481 (14.85)	.513 (14.84)			.648 (28.24)	.557 (17.57)
R^2	.448	.276	.247	.194	.420	.311
F	15.39	14.84	12.78	9.39	28.24	17.57

NOTE: p< .05 for underlined coefficients. F ratios in parentheses.

fertility and literacy variables are entered together as individual variables. This can be seen by comparing the results for the male group as a whole in Table 3.2, where the R^2 value was .431 to an R^2 value for males as a whole of .328 for the interaction term as the only explanatory variable. The joint effects of literacy and soil fertility suggest that it is possible that the relative depletion of persons from the more developed areas within the high soil fertility section of European Russia may have contributed to "backwardness" in southern Russia.

Returning to Table 3.2 for total sex groups, in the non-stepwise results, natural r remains negative although it loses its statistical significance. Literacy may be affecting the relationship of natural r to out-migration in a similar manner to its effect on soil fertility. For non-workers, soil fertility is positive and significant. Literacy is also positive for non-workers, significantly so for males, barely missing significance for females. The F value for the latter relationship of 3.82 falls slightly below the level of 4.11 that is necessary for significance at the 5 percent level.

Contrary to expectations, the coefficients for secondary industry become negative for workers, significantly so for females and almost significantly for males. The regression coefficients for non-workers for secondary industry are close to zero, while the correlation coefficient for secondary industry for male non-workers is significantly positive. In both the correlations and the regressions, the relation of secondary industry for workers was more negative (or less positive) for workers than for non-workers. One possible explanation is that if a person desiring wage work lives in an area that is fairly highly developed industrially, then he may have some tendency to stay there to seek work. Another possible explanation, though, especially when the destination is a developed industrial area, is that persons who intend to migrate in the company of non-working children or other non-working family members may be more willing to migrate with a family if they are from a fairly industrially developed area. However, for persons seeking wage work who migrate alone or in the company of others also seeking wage work, past exposure to industrially developed environments may be less crucial in the migration decision. It is possible that taking non-working spouses or wives along implies a greater commitment to the move than migrating alone. This is discussed more thoroughly in the chapter on Moscow and St. Petersburg.

Another factor affecting the regression coefficients for secondary industry is the positive relationship between secondary industry and literacy (correlated .678). Two strongly positively correlated variables entered jointly into the same multiple regression equation will create a tendency for the regression coefficients of the two variables to be negatively correlated. This phenomenon is the problem of multicollinearity. Although secondary industry and literacy are not so highly correlated that they definitely should not be entered into the same equation, the fairly strong correlations among the explanatory variables mean that although the regression results are informative, the correlation results are also important. Later chapters examine partial correlations that control for the effect of the distance between the origin and the destination.

In this chapter, the expectation that cultural modernization would be positively related to out-migration was given strong support in the results for literacy. Similarly, the negative or insignificant relationship of natural r to out-migration rates refutes the idea that population pressure is generally a strong positive cause of out-migration in societies at an early stage of modernization. The positive relationship of soil fertility to out-migration, especially for non-workers or in combination with literacy, was not expected. However, this finding suggests that under some conditions cultural development can overcome other factors affecting migration propensity. It is interesting that the interaction variable for soil fertility and literacy was not important for migration to specific destinations considered. This implies that the counterbalancing role of literacy for the effect of soil fertility was more important in determining a *general* propensity to leave one's place of birth than it was for determining migration to any particular destination. The conditions under which natural r can positively affect migration are investigated in the chapter on Asiatic Russia. The expectation that industrial development of the origin would be positively related to out-migration rates was given at best partial support. There was some indication that for non-workers this might be the case. However there was no support for this expectation for workers, and the relations for workers suggested that the opposite might be true. The relation of industrial modernization to migration is quite complex and is examined in more detail in the chapter on Moscow and St. Petersburg.

CHAPTER 4

Migration to Modern Urban Centers: Moscow and St. Petersburg Cities

Moscow and St. Petersburg cities were the most culturally and industrially modern locales in European Russia in 1897. Table 2.8 shows that they had a higher proportion of each sex in fairly modern occupations than any other detailed destination. Thus they will be used as the prime examples of modern destinations in this study.

It is not surprising that there was a high rate of participation in wage work in Moscow and St. Petersburg compared to the other destinations considered, since a fairly high rate would be expected simply because they were cities. However, the high incidence of participation in wage work and the relative modernity of the occupational distribution in the two great cities also appears when they are compared with the third largest city in European Russia in 1897, Odessa. Table 4.1 shows the distribution of the wage labor force in these three cities. It is clear that a higher proportion of each sex was engaged in wage work in either Moscow or St. Petersburg than in Odessa. Also a higher proportion of each sex was engaged in relatively modern jobs in the two great cities than in Odessa. This more modern occupational structure is seen in the higher proportion of each sex in secondary industry and the lower proportion in household service in Moscow or St. Petersburg compared to Odessa.

Populations in the two great cities were also more literate than was the population of Odessa. Table 4.2 shows the proportion of each city's population that was literate circa 1870. Thus even compared to the next largest city in European Russia, Moscow and St. Petersburg cities were distin-

TABLE 4.1

WORKERS AND SERVANTS RESIDENT IN MOSCOW, ST. PETERSBURG
OR ODESSA: 1897

	Moscow		St. Petersburg		Odessa	
	Male	Female	Male	Female	Male	Female
Population in Thousands	592	447	693	572	217	187
Population of Workers and Servants in Thousands	299	134	292	142	65	28
% of Population who were Workers or Servants	50.6%	30.1%	42.1%	24.7%	30.0%	15.0%
% Distribution of Workers and Servants						
Workers in Secondary Industry	59.5	33.2	50.4	24.2	40.6	13.7
Workers in Transportation, Communication or Commerce	21.0	6.2	21.5	3.1	19.7	5.8
Unskilled and Day Laborers	5.3	3.3	9.0	7.4	21.5	7.8
Servants in Administrative and Social Institutions	2.9	3.2	4.8	3.6	2.6	1.0
Household Servants	10.0	53.6	12.3	61.5	12.1	71.3
Other	1.3	.5	2.0	.2	3.5	.4
Total	100.0%	100.0%	100.0%	100.0%	100.0%	100.0%

guished by their level of development. Only the Baltic provinces had similarly high literacy levels.

THE UNCHANGING PATTERN OF MIGRATION TO THE GREAT CITIES

Although the 1897 Imperial Census was the first census of the Russian Empire, there were earlier censuses taken in some major cities. The first St. Petersburg City census was taken in 1869 (Russia 1872) and censuses were also taken in Moscow City in 1871 and 1882 (Moscow [City] Statisticheskii Otdel 1885-1886). These earlier urban censuses provide some information on the number and origins of migrants. The data can be used in combination with information on the population of provinces before 1897 in order to

TABLE 4.2

PERCENTAGE LITERATE IN ST. PETERSBURG, MOSCOW AND ODESSA CIRCA 1870

City	Year	Male	Female
St. Petersburg	1869	62	46
Moscow	1871	50	34
Odessa	1873	36	22

determine the similarity of the migration pattern to the two great cities in 1897 with the migration pattern to these cities at an earlier time.

For each city, the pattern of migration changed very little in the twenty or thirty years before the 1897 census. Considering both sexes together, the correlation of migration rates (on forty-one provinces) for migration to St. Petersburg in 1869 and 1897 is .963. The correlation for migration to Moscow in 1882 and 1897 is .961.[1] Thus although the volume of migration increased considerably over time, the relation among the migration rates from various provinces remained substantially unchanged.

Table 4.3 shows the percentage of the population who were migrants and the total population in thousands in Moscow City and in St. Petersburg City for various dates from the 1880s to the early twentieth century (Rashin 1956: 86-91, 138, 144). Although the cities grew rapidly, substantially due to migration, the proportion migrant remained at a

[1] For province A, the migration rate to St. Petersburg 1869 had as numerator the number of peasants stating province A as their origin who lived in St. Petersburg in 1869; the denominator was the population of province A in 1863 in thousands (Rashin 1956: 44-45). For province A, the migration rate to Moscow 1882 had as numerator the number of persons stating province A as origin who lived in Moscow in 1882; the denominator was the number of persons estimated to have lived in province A in 1882 in thousands. The population of province A in 1882 was estimated from an exponential interpolation between the population of province A in 1863 and the population of province A in 1885 (ibid.).

TABLE 4.3

PERCENTAGE MIGRANT AND TOTAL POPULATION OF MOSCOW AND ST. PETERSBURG
CITIES FROM THE 1880S TO THE EARLY TWENTIETH CENTURY

	Moscow			St. Petersburg	
Date	% Migrant	Population in Thousands	Date	% Migrant	Population in Thousands
1882	74	754	1881	71	861
1897	74	1039	1897	70	1265
1902	73	1175	1900	68	1440
1912	71	1616	1910	68	1906

consistently high level throughout this period. Since the children of migrants who were born in a city are natives of that city rather than migrants, it is clear that migration rates were very high even before the 1880s.

This unchanging pattern of migration to the two great cities is significant for a number of reasons, even though the volume of migration increased with time. First, it helps establish the important position that Moscow and St. Petersburg had held in European Russia for a long time. Second, it raises questions about the meaning of premodern and early modern development and its effects on the extent of success of the society in later adaptation to modern conditions.

The extent to which the nature of premodern development is related to the ease of adaptation to modern conditions has been a concern of several recent studies of Russia (Coale, Anderson, and Härm 1979; Black et al. 1975; Rozman 1976). The similarity of the pattern of origins of migration in 1897 to the pattern twenty or thirty years earlier leads to speculation about how long a similar pattern, albeit at a lower volume, had persisted. It is possible that even in 1869 or 1883 differential modernization of various places of origin determined the pattern of migration to the great cities. Recall that the relative pattern of development of Russia at the end of the nineteenth century was similar to the development pattern in the mid-nineteenth century. The correlation between workers per thousand population 1860 and workers in secondary industry per thousand population 1897 is .803, and the correlation between percentage of military recruits literate 1873-1884 and percentage military recruits literate 1904 is .832. However, another possible interpretation is that long-standing differences in European Russia that were not originally related to differential modernity may have differentially predisposed persons from various areas to migrate to the two great cities even as early as 1870. Specifically, this line of reasoning refers to the differences in climate and soil type that may have led to differences in work organization under serfdom and later to regional differences in the development of modern industry. Chapter 2 discusses these relations. Sometimes a society's traditional social patterns, such as importance of achievement criteria or regional specialization, coincide with types of social patterns common in modern or modernizing societies. Such societies may have a better chance of successfully modernizing than societies where traditional social patterns are radically different from those found in more modern societies.

The importance of these traditional patterns becomes evident when we examine a study that was made of human fertility in Russia. Coale, Anderson, and Härm (1979) found that in late nineteenth-century European Russia, there was a close relationship between female literacy and the average age of female marriage: the higher the literacy, the higher the age of female marriage. A rise in age of female marriage is a change that is often supposed to accompany modernization. However, the study found no relation between the change in the proportion of females literate and the change in the age of female marriage. Thus it seemed unlikely that the differences among the age of female marriage in various provinces resulted from the differential progress modernization had made in various provinces. Rather, it seemed more likely that these differences in female marriage age and in literacy were related to long-standing differences among areas that were not necessarily directly related to socioeconomic modernization.

It seems that the regional pattern of industry in nineteenth-century Russia changed in a manner that brought it into coincidence with longstanding regional differences in the organization of work. In the first half of the nineteenth century, the industries in European Russia that most heavily employed modern production methods were the cotton and beet sugar industries. The modern beet sugar industry was originally concentrated in the south, in the Ukraine (Yatsunsky 1974; Fedor 1975). However, by the 1860s, modern industry had shifted its focus northward to those areas where cottage industry had long been established. It would be interesting to know how the migration pattern in the 1870s or the 1890s differed from that in the 1840s. However, that is the subject of another study.[2]

[2] Kabuzan (1971) presents data for the early nineteenth century on the number of in-migrants and the number of out-migrants by province of European Russia. In an attempt to check the quality of that data, this researcher correlated the amount of net migration implied by the gross flows in and out of each province with an estimate of population change due to migration for each province. In order to obtain an estimate of population change due to migration, the difference between Rashin's (1956) estimated populations for provinces at two dates and the change in population size that would be implied by an estimate of the crude birth rate, crude death rate, and the population size at the first date was calculated. The number of persons who, according to Kabuzan, would have been net migrants was unrelated to the estimate of population change due to migration from the birth and death rates. Since these two quantities should have been closely related if both sets of data were accurate, and since the two quantities were unrelated, it was decided that the quality of

In addition to its obvious substantive interest, the similarity of the pattern of origins of migration to the two great cities for a substantial time period before the 1897 census is important for methodological reasons. Lifetime migration represents the cumulation of past migration patterns over a considerable period of time. Substantial change in the pattern of migration over time may make lifetime migration difficult to interpret, since lifetime migration is an average of these changing patterns. The cumulation of different patterns may lead to misinterpretation of the factors related to migration in any given time period. However, a similarity among migration rates at times separated by as much as twenty years makes it unlikely that the relative pattern (as opposed to the absolute level) of migration among origins has changed considerably. Evidence of such an unchanging pattern indicates that it is fairly safe to interpret lifetime migration patterns as if they referred to the pattern of migration during a particular period of time, although the exact extent of the period of reference is unknown. Migration to Asiatic Russia displayed a large change in migration patterns over time. Thus it may be misleading to interpret lifetime migration to Asiatic Russia in 1897 as if it represented the migration pattern in any given time period. Chapter 5 discusses this situation in some detail.

Ecological Effects of Literacy on Migration

For 1897, the only information available in the census on the characteristics of migrants from particular provinces is their sex and whether in 1897 they were engaged in wage

---

the data was too uncertain to warrant further use. If the data quality had appeared satisfactory, then Kabuzan's data could have been used to examine labor shifts among geographical regions in the first half of the nineteenth century.

work. Thus from the 1897 Imperial Census alone, it is not possible to determine the proportion of migrants who were literate from any particular province. In particular, if that census were the only relevant data source, it would be impossible to determine whether a finding of high migration rates from highly literate provinces was due to a general propensity for persons, whether literate or illiterate, to migrate from highly literate provinces or whether higher migration rates of literates than illiterates on an individual level completely accounted for the positive association between migration rates and an indicator of the level of literacy in provinces. This study supposes that the ecological effects of a high literacy level on all provincial residents may well induce a propensity to migrate even among illiterates. Many other studies (Greenwood 1969; Levy and Wadycki 1973) have interpreted a positive association between migration rates and literacy levels as an indication of the greater propensity of literates than illiterates to migrate, even though researchers have not usually examined their data to determine whether this supposition was valid.

The 1869 St. Petersburg City Census (Russia 1872) presents data that can be used to address this question. The census presents a table referring only to peasants,[3] which cross-classifies migrants to St. Petersburg by sex, province of origin, and age. The age breakdown is determined by whether or not the person was at least seven years of age, and for persons aged at least seven, there is a further break-

[3] It is somewhat fortunate that the data refer only to peasants. If gentry and nobility had been included, the interpretation that migration before 1869 had the same general character as migration before 1897 would have been more questionable. Since the absolute number of migrants from some provinces was small, if gentry had been included in the data, the phenomenon of geographical circulation of elites (Black et al. 1975) could have confounded the results.

down by literacy. Examination of these data can indicate whether migration rates from provinces with a high level of literacy are simply due to a greater propensity of the literate than the illiterate to migrate. Table 4.4 shows the correlations among migration rates to St. Petersburg City for 1869 and the proportion of migrants who were literate by province of origin. It also shows the correlations between the migration rates and various explanatory variables. The correlations for migration rates of the population aged at least seven years show the predicted pattern for migration to a relatively modern destination. Migration rates are higher from more literate origins and lower from origins with a heavy involvement in traditional agriculture or with a high

TABLE 4.4

CORRELATIONS FOR MIGRATION TO ST. PETERSBURG CITY: 1869 (ON 41 PROVINCES)

	Male 7+ Migration Rate	Female 7+ Migration ·Rate	Proportion Male Migrants 7+ Literate	Proportion Female Migrants 7+ Literate
Correlations with Explanatory Variables				
Soil	-.507	-.669	.172	.255
Lit7483	.806	.686	-.071	-.396
Work60	-.087	-.118	.080	-.069
Nat r61	-.543	-.550	.175	.415
lnDistSt.P	-.463	-.673	.426	.418
Correlations Among Migration Rates				
Male 7+ Migration Rate	1.000	.842	-.122	-.367
Female 7+ Migration Rate		1.000	-.317	-.460
Proportion Male Migrants 7+ Literate			1.000	.704
Proportion Female Migrants 7+ Literate				1.000

NOTE: p<.05 for underlined coefficients, two-tailed tests.

rate of natural increase. Migration rates are lower the farther the origin was from St. Petersburg. The only unexpected finding is the negative correlation between migration and the proportion of the population who were workers in 1860, although the correlations are insignificant. The correlations were quite similar to those for migration to St. Petersburg in 1897, as shown in Table 4.5

The relations between the explanatory variables and the proportion of migrants by province of origin who were literate are quite different from the relations for overall migration rates. If the ratio of the migration rates of literate and illiterate persons did not differ among provinces, then the correlation between the proportion of migrants from a province who were literate and the proportion of military recruits from a province who were literate should be 1.000. A special case of this would be if all literate persons everywhere experienced the same migration rate and all illiterate persons everywhere experienced the same migration rate, although this would be a different rate from that of literate persons. Even allowing for measurement error and other confounding factors, if the ecological literacy rate of a province did not affect the differential migration of literates as compared to illiterates, then the correlation between the proportion literate who migrated to St. Petersburg City and the proportion of military recruits who were literate should at least be strong and positive.

This is not the case. Columns 3 and 4 of Table 4.4 show a negative correlation between the proportion of military recruits who were literate and the proportion of migrants to St. Petersburg City who were literate for each sex. This correlation is statistically significant for females. The finding of negative or insignificant correlations between the proportion of migrants who were literate and an estimate of the proportion literate in the province of origin is consistent with the interpretation that illiterate persons in the provinces with a higher level of literacy were relatively more likely to migrate than were illiterates in less literate provinces.[4] This finding supports the interpretation of characteristics of provinces as representing ecological conditions that affect the behavior of persons in those provinces apart from the individual characteristics of persons. This finding also counters the interpretation of aggregate characteristics as simply representing a summary measure of the distribution of the individual characteristics in the population.

The significant positive correlations between the proportion of migrants who were literate and the natural logarithm of the distance to St. Petersburg in hundreds of miles also suggest that long distances were less of a hindrance to the migration of literate than illiterate persons. One overall interpretation of these findings is that if a person has some characteristic such as literacy that might make him view migration as a realistic possibility regardless of what those around him think, then the distance to the potential destination may be relatively unimportant. However, if a person does not possess a characteristic such as literacy that might predispose him to migrate, then the characteristics of those around him are quite important, and long distance may be viewed as a major obstacle to migration.

MIGRATION TO MOSCOW AND ST. PETERSBURG
CITIES: 1897

Moscow and St. Petersburg were the most modern destinations in European Russia in 1897, but there were differ-

---

[4] The problem with the literacy data is that there is no indication of how many peasants from any given province acquired literacy before migration to St. Petersburg and how many acquired literacy after migration. There is even no information on what proportion of all literate peasants who had migrated to St. Petersburg acquired literacy after migration.

ences between them. On balance, Moscow was more of an industrial center, while St. Petersburg was more of a cultural center. Tables 4.1 and 4.2 suggest these differences. It is clear that the population of St. Petersburg was more literate, while the wage labor force in Moscow had a more modern occupational distribution.

Even though the two great cities were different in these respects, their similarities were such that when compared to the rest of European Russia they can be considered as alternative destinations for migration. Gilbert Rozman (1976: 218) examined marketing relations in premodern China, Japan, and Russia, noting that when two cities similar in size and in distance to Moscow and St. Petersburg were found in premodern China or Japan, a distinct hinterland for marketing existed for each city. However, in the case of Moscow and St. Petersburg in the late eighteenth century, the two cities seemed to share a single, large, well-integrated hinterland that could not easily be logically divided into two separate parts, one serving each city. Thus marketing relations were more integrated for the two great Russian cities than was the case for other similarly paired cities in premodern Japan or China.

Migration to Moscow and St. Petersburg can be investigated either by examining migration to each city separately or by considering migration where the destination was either of the two cities. Table 4.5 shows the correlations between the explanatory variables and the migration rates to the two cities separately and considered together as one destination. The form of the rates is similar to the out-migration rates discussed in the previous chapter. For Moscow City, for instance, the male migration rate from Vladimir province would be the number of males born in Vladimir who in 1897 lived in Moscow City, per thousand males born in Vladimir who lived anywhere in the Russian Empire. For the migration rate to Moscow or St. Petersburg cities, the

TABLE 4.5

CORRELATIONS AND PARTIAL CORRELATIONS FOR MIGRATION TO MOSCOW AND ST. PETERSBURG CITIES: 1897 (ON 41 PROVINCES)

	St. Petersburg						Moscow					
	M	F	MW	FW	MNW	FNW	M	F	MW	FW	MNW	FNW
Correlations												
Soil	-.482	-.681	-.697	-.700	-.523	-.665	-.215	-.190	-.168	-.124	-.249	-.200
Lit7483	.772	.656	.592	.480	.792	.716	.563	.546	.454	.417	.600	.560
WorkSec97	.291	.158	.095	.004	.352	.219	.542	.587	.350	.297	.686	.746
Nat r8185	-.470	-.457	-.444	-.404	-.457	-.477	-.369	-.353	-.301	-.286	-.394	-.363
Dist	-.585	-.735	-.758	-.797	-.478	-.700	-.780	-.782	-.743	-.729	-.689	-.731
Partial Correlations Controlling for Distance Measure												
Soil	-.321	-.384	-.401	-.381	-.314	-.376	-.123	-.093	-.054	.009	-.177	-.104
Lit7483	.721	.577	.478	.284	.745	.661	.243	.210	.068	.016	.357	.267
WorkSec97	.284	.121	.025	-.132	.345	.206	.223	.308	-.098	-.175	.510	.610
Nat r8185	-.273	-.187	-.154	-.056	-.300	-.245	.038	.069	.122	.132	-.080	.004
Mean	14.477	8.460	70.846	57.737	7.027	5.602	8.726	4.590	36.112	41.235	4.011	2.484
s.d.	25.280	14.135	118.803	103.629	12.176	8.893	16.754	8.826	63.366	81.114	8.484	4.870

Table 4.5 (Continued)

| | Moscow or St. Petersburg | | | | | | Moscow/Moscow or St. Petersburg | | | | | |
	M	F	MW	FW	MNW	FNW	M	F	MW	FW	MNW	FNW
Correlations												
Soil	-.535	-.639	-.658	-.612	-.496	-.646	.517	.533	.678	.659	.352	.486
Lit7483	.846	.800	.700	.619	.863	.843	-.099	-.085	-.338	-.254	.031	-.049
WorkSec97	.480	.420	.236	.182	.591	.524	.320	.325	.115	.174	.379	.365
Nat r8185	-.528	-.541	-.506	-.482	-.522	-.563	.028	.076	.344	.326	-.091	.023
Dist	-.727	-.782	-.743	-.790	-.634	-.752	-.656	-.778	-.605	-.716	-.567	-.758
Partial Correlations on Distance Measure												
Soil	-.411	-.597	-.610	-.554	-.360	-.594	.323	.317	.566	.534	.126	.239
Lit7483	.766	.687	.500	.338	.790	.784	-.245	-.296	-.526	-.500	-.052	-.227
WorkSec97	.259	.133	-.153	-.304	.449	.325	.089	.031	-.169	-.169	.206	.110
Nat r8185	-.185	-.166	-.132	-.042	-.240	-.230	.050	.139	.443	.480	-.101	.052
Mean	23.202	13.049	106.958	98.971	11.038	8.086	395.801	405.125	533.660	560.065	329.972	349.651
s.d.	5.342	17.682	142.053	134.912	17.079	10.665	226.305	219.401	286.006	278.668	216.210	202.479

NOTE: p< .05 for underlined coefficients, two-tailed tests.

numerator would be the number of males born in Vladimir who in 1897 lived in either Moscow or St. Petersburg cities, and the denominator would be the same as the denominator for migration to Moscow City.

For the individual cities, the distance measure used is the natural logarithm of the distance from a point centrally located in the province of birth to the given city in hundreds of miles. For migration to Moscow *or* St. Petersburg cities considered together, the distance measure used is the natural logarithm of the distance in hundreds of miles to the closer of the two cities.[5]

As shown in Table 4.5, the correlations between explanatory variables and migration rates to the two cities separately are generally as expected. Migration rates are low from high soil fertility provinces, significantly so for migration to St. Petersburg. For all groups, for each city, migration rates are positively related to the level of literacy at the origin. Also, consistent with expectations, migration rates are positively related to the proportion of the popula-

---

[5] The natural logarithm of the average of the distances to the two great cities was also tried as a distance measure, but with little effect on the results. The distance measure chosen had a somewhat larger correlation with migration rates than did the natural logarithm of the average distance. Use of the natural logarithm of the distance to the closer of the two cities caused the relation of the non-distance explanatory variables with the migration rates to be somewhat weaker than in the results using the natural logarithm of the average of the distance to the two cities. Conceptually, of course, the natural logarithm of the distance to the closer of the two cities is a more proper measure. A person could live in Ryazan province, which is very close to Moscow, on the far side of Moscow from St. Petersburg. If Moscow and St. Petersburg cities can be considered as alternative destinations, then the relevant fact about distance to the two great cities for the potential migrant from Ryazan is that Moscow is quite close rather than that Moscow and St. Petersburg *on average* are fairly distant.

tion in the province of origin in secondary industry for all groups for migration to Moscow except for female workers and for male non-worker migrants to St. Petersburg. Natural r at the origin is negatively related to migration propensity for every group for each city. As is usual for migration, the rates for all groups for each city tend to be higher the closer the origin is to the city considered as destination.

The correlations for migration to Moscow or St. Petersburg cities considered together as a single destination are generally similar to those for the cites considered separately, except that the correlations of literacy with migration rates are larger (more positive) for the cities considered together than separately. The higher correlations for literacy when the cities are considered together supports the interpretation that Moscow and St. Petersburg were alternative destinations.

Maps 4.1 to 4.3 show the male migration rate to Moscow City, St. Petersburg City, and Moscow or St. Petersburg cities, respectively. The effect of distance on migration is quite apparent. Migration rates were generally higher to St. Petersburg than to Moscow. This is shown by the mean migration rates at the bottom of Table 4.5. However, St. Petersburg drew more migrants from the area around Moscow than Moscow drew migrants from near St. Petersburg. Migration to Moscow was more concentrated in the ring of provinces around Moscow province than migration to St. Petersburg was concentrated in provinces that were very near that city.

The pattern of origins shown in Maps 4.1-4.3 for the total male group is quite similar to what would be shown for the other sex and labor force groups. For migration to Moscow, the lowest correlation with the male migration rate was .914, for St. Petersburg the lowest was .734, and for Moscow and St. Petersburg considered together, it was .792.

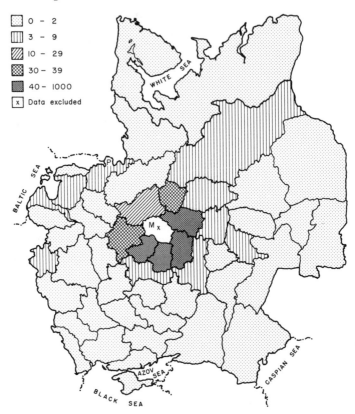

0 – 2
3 – 9
10 – 29
30 – 39
40 – 1000
[x] Data excluded

MAP 4.1 Male Lifetime Migration Rate to Moscow City: 1897

For migration to Moscow, the correlations among the migration rates showed that work status was more predictive of migration than was sex. This finding parallels that for general out-migration. The correlation between migration rates to Moscow City for workers of each sex was .980; for non-workers by sex it was .933. These correlations were higher than the correlations with the group of the same sex and the other work status. Migration to St. Petersburg and to the two cities combined showed a different pattern. For

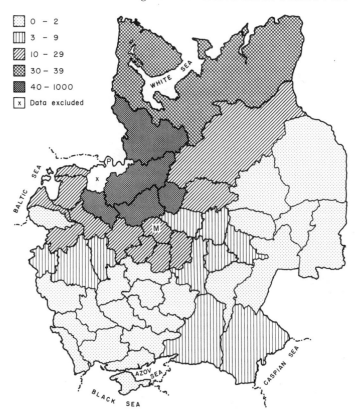

::::	0 - 2
‖‖‖	3 - 9
▨	10 - 29
▩	30 - 39
■	40 - 1000
x	Data excluded

MAP 4.2 Male Lifetime Migration Rate to St. Petersburg City: 1897

St. Petersburg and the two cities, there was some indication that the migration of males seeking wage work was a major determining factor of whether other persons migrated. The correlation for St. Petersburg for male and female non-workers was .863, but it was .941 when female non-workers and male workers were compared. Similarly, for both cities combined, the correlation between migration rates for male and female non-workers was .875, while the correlation between female non-workers and male workers

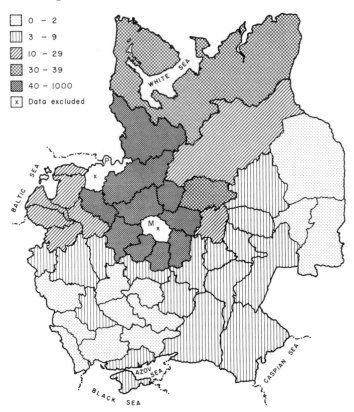

☐ 0 – 2
▥ 3 – 9
▨ 10 – 29
▩ 30 – 39
■ 40 – 1000
x Data excluded

MAP 4.3 Male Lifetime Migration Rate to Moscow or St. Petersburg
  Cities: 1897

was .912. In all cases, the correlation between migration
rates for male and female workers was higher than the correlation between workers of a given sex and non-workers of
the same sex.

As Chapter 2 indicates, provinces close to Moscow and
St. Petersburg cities had high literacy levels and high proportions of the population engaged in secondary industry.
Literacy of military recruits 1874-1883 and the logarithm
of distance to the closer of Moscow or St. Petersburg cities

are correlated at $-.568$, and the correlation between this distance measure and the secondary industry variable is $-.442$. Even if persons migrated randomly, persons from highly literate provinces and persons from provinces where a high proportion of the population was engaged in secondary industry would have been disproportionately found in Moscow and St. Petersburg cities.

In order to take the possible mechanical effect of distance into account, partial correlations controlling for the relevant distance measure were computed. The results of a partial correlation can be interpreted similarly to correlations. However, the partial correlations control for the relationship between the variables of interest and the distance measure. The partial correlations appear in the lower part of Table 4.5. The relationship of literacy to migration generally remains strong and positive, despite the negative relations between literacy and distance to either city. Only for Moscow City does controlling for distance eliminate the relationship of literacy to migration for most groups. The literacy results for the two cities combined are stronger than for St. Petersburg alone, which is consistent with the notion that for some purposes the two cities were a common destination. For St. Petersburg and for the two cities combined, the correlations with soil fertility remain negative and significant. This finding is consistent with the hypothesis that places with a heavy involvement in traditional agriculture do not tend to produce persons willing to migrate to modern destinations. The generally negative, but insignificant, correlations between soil fertility and migration to Moscow suggest that traditional agriculture may induce more reluctance to migrate to culturally modern places than to industrially modern places.

Migration to Moscow and St. Petersburg can also be examined through the use of multiple regressions, as was done for out-migration generally in Chapter 3. Stepwise and non-stepwise standardized multiple regression coefficients appear in Table 4.6. The R^2 values for the two cities combined are in every case higher than the R^2 values for any particular group for either city separately. This difference suggests that considering the cities together provides a more accurate total picture of migration than does considering them separately. If radically different factors determined migration to each of the two cities, then combining the cities together and entering the same variables as independent variables in a regression would only increase the amount of seemingly random variability in the data and would lower the R^2 values (the proportion of the variance in the dependent variable explained). All of the R^2 values are quite high, and all of the equations are significant as a whole. Literacy again appears quite important for St. Petersburg and for the two cities combined. For Moscow, distance is important in every case, but the only other variable that is significant in the regressions is secondary industry for non-workers. The relative inefficacy of the explanatory variable relationships for Moscow considered alone is thought to be related to the contention that Moscow and St. Petersburg were alternative destinations for many purposes. As indicated in Maps 4.1-4.4, St. Petersburg drew heavily from provinces near Moscow. When migration to Moscow is considered alone, persons from provinces between St. Petersburg and Moscow may have chosen St. Petersburg because it was relatively close, while otherwise they might have migrated to Moscow. The next section examines the determinants of choice of destination between the two great cities.

ALLOCATION OF MIGRANTS BETWEEN MOSCOW AND ST. PETERSBURG CITIES

If Moscow and St. Petersburg cities were alternative destinations for some purposes, then the migration decision

(*Continued, p. 112*)

TABLE 4.6

STEPWISE AND NON-STEPWISE STANDARDIZED MULTIPLE REGRESSIONS FOR MOSCOW AND ST. PETERSBURG CITIES: 1897 (ON 41 PROVINCES)

	St. Petersburg						Moscow					
	M	F	MW	FW	MNW	FNW	M	F	MW	FW	MNW	FNW
Stepwise Regressions												
Soil				-.307 (6.47)								
Lit7483	.907 (51.09)	.715 (34.30)	.643 (26.27)		1.026 (69.92)	.792 (44.76)					.441 (13.37)	.497 (22.54)
WorkSec97	-.351 (9.07)	-.377 (11.30)	-.397 (11.87)		-.344 (7.87)	-.361 (11.04)						
Nat r8185												
Dist	-.254 (7.31)	-.484 (28.74)	-.538 (33.68)	-.595 (24.29)		-.417 (22.72)	-.780 (60.74)	-.695 (31.78)	-.743 (48.08)	-.729 (44.26)	-.448 (13.80)	-.460 (19.35)
R²	.746	.765	.751	.689	.691	.779	.609	.655	.552	.532	.611	.708
F	36.21	40.05	37.24	42.06	42.57	43.47	60.74	23.39	48.08	44.26	29.87	46.02
Non-Stepwise Regressions												
Soil	.162 (1.53)	-.025 (.04)	-.110 (.69)	-.191 (2.05)	.191 (1.80)	.035 (.08)	.011 (.01)	.010 (.01)	.016 (.01)	.062 (.18)	-.019 (.02)	-.033 (.08)
Lit7483	1.069 (45.85)	.753 (23.36)	.615 (14.82)	.402 (6.32)	1.125 (43.59)	.869 (33.40)	.219 (1.23)	.139 (.51)	.245 (1.29)	.270 (1.53)	.127 (.38)	-.043 (.06)
WorkSec97	-.360 (9.58)	-.366 (10.15)	-.378 (10.29)	-.366 (0.62)	-.317 (6.37)	-.357 (10.33)	.082 (.32)	.189 (1.75)	-.169 (1.14)	-.238 (2.19)	.385 (6.48)	.533 (16.67)
Nat r8185	.169 (2.17)	.108 (.91)	.060 (.27)	.026 (.05)	.171 (1.92)	.127 (1.36)	.142 (1.14)	.148 (1.29)	.169 (1.36)	.161 (1.20)	.075 (.30)	.101 (.71)
Dist	-.375 (9.86)	-.501 (18.04)	-.503 (17.26)	-.559 (21.33)	-.262 (4.11)	-.468 (16.86)	-.686 (27.05)	-.677 (27.37)	-.786 (29.88)	-.800 (30.09)	-.442 (10.39)	-.509 (18.47)
R²	.766	.772	.760	.760	.727	.787	.648	.641	.582	.571	.620	.717
F	22.88	23.68	22.15	22.15	18.63	25.91	12.90	13.67	9.31	11.41	11.41	17.69

Table 4.6 (Continued)

Stepwise Regressions

	Moscow or St. Petersburg						Moscow/Moscow or St. Petersburg					
	M	F	MW	FW	MNW	FNW	M	F	MW	FW	MNW	FNW
Soil	.773 (58.34)		-.241 (7.16)	-.233 (7.09)		-.182 (5.24)	.445 (9.00)	.224 (4.23)	.507 (17.94)	.318 (7.91)		
Lit7483		.694 (49.02)	(18.83)	-.446 (22.12)	.742 (62.93)	.521 (34.00)						
WorkSec97	-.213 (5.24)	-.277 (9.24)	-.428 (19.21)				.306 (4.53)					
Nat r8185										.218 (4.72)		
Dist	-.382 (21.18)	-.510 (39.40)	-.536 (40.56)	-.674 (67.92)	-.213 (5.17)	-.388 (25.66)	-.331 (4.52)	-.675 (38.49)	-.372 (9.66)	-.573 (29.63)	-.567 (18.45)	-.758 (52.81)
R^2	.829	.836	.830	.839	.775	.854	.547	.644	.569	.691	.321	.575
F	59.90	62.91	43.88	47.05	65.42	71.87	14.76	34.41	25.08	27.57	18.46	32.81

Non-Stepwise Regressions

	Moscow or St. Petersburg						Moscow/Moscow or St. Petersburg					
	M	F	MW	FW	MNW	FNW	M	F	MW	FW	MNW	FNW
Soil	.053 (.38)	-.156 (3.48)	-.234 (6.72)	-.226 (6.72)	.074 (.52)	-.150 (3.40)	.276 (2.04)	.162 (.98)	.401 (5.36)	.339 (4.80)	.182 (.67)	.119 (.49)
Lit7483	.898 (49.32)	.639 (27.56)	.588 (19.64)	.454 (12.53)	.870 (33.29)	.657 (29.95)	-.322 (2.04)	-.294 (2.37)	-.244 (1.45)	-.148 (.67)	-.282 (1.18)	-.350 (3.09)
WorkSec97	-.237 (6.34)	-.238 (7.09)	-.434 (19.81)	-.453 (23.07)	-.039 (.12)	-.105 (1.41)	.409 (6.01)	.310 (4.83)	.339 (5.12)	.272 (4.13)	.413 (4.60)	.361 (6.01)
Nat r8185	.179 (3.85)	.136 (2.46)	.101 (1.13)	.111 (1.47)	.138 (1.64)	.116 (1.84)	-.097 (.45)	-.028 (.05)	.192 (2.19)	.230 (3.95)	-.156 (.88)	-.080 (.39)
Dist	-.446 (26.42)	-.545 (43.68)	-.571 (40.10)	-.712 (66.80)	-.265 (6.73)	-.437 (28.76)	-.408 (6.14)	-.618 (19.59)	-.321 (4.72)	-.476 (12.98)	-.355 (3.48)	-.605 (17.29)
R^2	.920	.862	.835	.846	.787	.865	.570	.691	.653	.724	.427	.664
F	38.78	43.61	35.45	38.43	25.93	44.96	9.27	15.63	13.19	18.32	5.22	13.84

NOTE: $p < .05$ for underlined coefficients. F ratios in parentheses.

process might be conceptualized as follows: a person may first decide he wants to migrate to a major urban modern destination, that is, Moscow or St. Petersburg cities; only then may he decide which destination to choose. If this alternative destination model is accurate, an important factor influencing the choice of destination should be the relative proximity of each to his origin. This relative distance concept can be expressed as the percentage by which one city is closer than the other. Specifically it can be expressed as the distance to St. Petersburg City divided by the average of the distance to Moscow City and to St. Petersburg City.

The relative propensity of migrants from a given province to choose Moscow rather than St. Petersburg can be expressed as the number of persons born in province A who in 1897 lived in Moscow City per thousand persons born in province A who in 1897 lived in either Moscow or St. Petersburg. This is essentially a conditional probability, conditioned on the persons having migrated to *either* Moscow or St. Petersburg. Map 4.4 shows the proportion of male migrants to Moscow or St. Petersburg who migrated to Moscow.

If each city's relative proximity was important in the decision of which destination to choose, then the migration variable just described and the relative distance variable should be negatively related. Table. 4.5 shows the correlations between the allocational migration rate and the explanatory variables, including the relative distance variable. As expected, the relative proximity of each city was important for all groups. From the correlations, soil fertility was positively related to migrating to Moscow rather than to St. Petersburg. This is not surprising, since Moscow was south of St. Petersburg and closer to the higher soil fertility area. In the partial correlations, though, the positive relation with soil fertility remains. This again suggests that persons

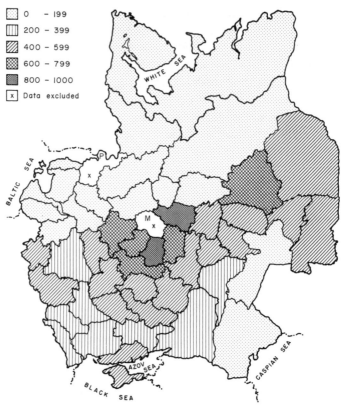

MAP 4.4 Male Lifetime Migration Rate to Moscow Per Thousand Migrants to Moscow or St. Petersburg Cities: 1897

from areas where traditional agriculture is important may be more willing to migrate to an industrial destination than to a cultural destination. Although natural r was not a significant factor for migration to Moscow considered alone, it seems that persons from provinces where population pressure was high were more willing to migrate to an industrially modern destination than to a culturally modern destination.

Table 4.6 presents the regression results for migration to

Moscow given the migrant went to either Moscow or St. Petersburg. In the stepwise regressions, soil fertility as a positive differentiating factor for migration to the two cities again appears. In the non-stepwise results, it is most interesting that for each group, the secondary industrial development of the origin is positively related to migrants choosing Moscow City rather than St. Petersburg City. Recall that the industrial development of the origin was not the expected strong positive influence on migration to modern destinations, except for persons who did not hold wage work jobs in 1897. However, it does seem to have some importance in determining the migrants' choice among various types of modern destinations. In the non-stepwise results in Table 4.6, literacy of the origin is negatively, although insignificantly, related to choosing Moscow rather than St. Petersburg.

MIGRATION TO MOSCOW OR ST. PETERSBURG CITIES AS COMPARED TO GENERAL OUT-MIGRATION

Generally, provinces with high rates of out-migration also had high rates of migration to Moscow or St. Petersburg cities. The correlation between the out-migration rate for a particular group and the migration rate to Moscow or St. Petersburg cities was positive and significant at the 5 percent level for all groups except female non-workers. One may ask whether the pattern of origins of migrants to Moscow City or St. Petersburg City is the same as the pattern when one considers only the universe of out-migrants. That is, a person may first decide to migrate out of his province of birth and may only then decide what destination to choose. One can ask what the determinants of choice of destination were for those persons who migrated out of their province of birth. It was clear from Chapter 3 that certain variables such as the literacy level of a province were strongly related to the propensity of persons from a given province to migrate out of the province. It is possible that a very different pattern of origins would appear if one considered, say, the migration rate to Moscow or St. Petersburg where the denominator was only persons who were out-migrants rather than considering migration to the two great cities where the denominator of the rate was all persons born in the province of origin.

This section considers the following migration rate. For province A, the numerator is the number of persons born in province A who in 1897 lived in either Moscow City or St. Petersburg City. The denominator is the number of persons in thousands who were born in province A and in 1897 lived anywhere in the Russian Empire *except* province A. Map 4.5 shows this migration variable for males. It does look much like Map 4.3, which showed the migration rate to the two great cities considering both migrants from provinces and those who remained in the province of birth. Table 4.7 shows the correlations and partial correlations for this variable. The distance variable is the natural logarithm of the distance to the closer of Moscow or St. Petersburg in hundreds of miles. The relations are quite similar to those in Table 4.5 for migration in Moscow or St. Petersburg. One difference is the stronger negative relationship with soil fertility in Table 4.7. The relationship with literacy is also somewhat stronger than in Table 4.5. Thus the same factors that were generally related to migrating to Moscow or St. Petersburg were also those factors related to choosing Moscow or St. Petersburg rather than other possible destinations. The somewhat stronger relations when only migrants are considered are related to the very different characteristics of origins of migrants to Asiatic Russia as compared to Moscow and St. Petersburg. Chapter 5 compares

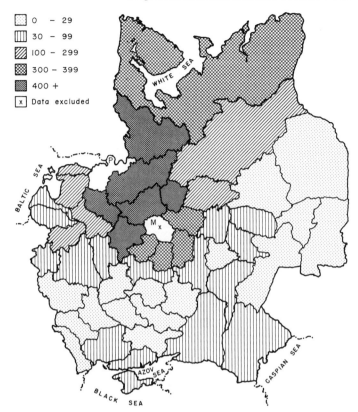

MAP 4.5 Male Lifetime Migration Rate to Moscow or St. Petersburg
Per Thousand Out-Migrants from Province of Birth: 1897

migration to Asiatic Russia and its changing nature over
time to migration to Moscow or St. Petersburg.

CONCLUSIONS

In this chapter a number of significant features of migration to European Russia's two great cities were established.
Evidence was presented to indicate that the relative pattern

TABLE 4.7

MIGRATION TO MOSCOW OR ST. PETERSBURG CITIES PER THOUSAND MIGRANTS
OUT OF THE PROVINCE OF BIRTH: 1897 (ON 41 PROVINCES)

	M	F	MW	FW	MNW	FNW
Correlations						
Soil	-.729	-.751	-.738	-.727	-.709	-.752
Lit7483	.807	.772	.740	.725	.865	.800
WorkSec97	.394	.385	.301	.315	.518	.445
Nat r8185	-.562	-.562	-.544	-.542	-.567	-.572
Dist	-.737	-.732	-.723	-.779	-.691	-.695
Partial Correlations Controlling for Distance Measure						
Soil	-.722	-.753	-.728	-.747	-.670	-.736
Lit7483	.699	.636	.578	.547	.794	.684
WorkSec97	.113	.101	-.029	-.051	.328	.214
Nat r8185	-.240	-.243	-.216	-.170	-.278	-.284
Mean	161.166	152.174	234.331	263.874	111.206	119.353
s.d.	190.090	190.837	264.413	289.477	132.849	152.073

NOTE: p<.05 for underlined coefficients, two-tailed tests.

of migration to each city by province of origin had not changed considerably in the last twenty years of the nineteenth century. This supported the interpretation of lifetime migration rates as if they referred to some period of migration. Examination of evidence on literacy of migrants from the 1869 St. Petersburg Census in comparison with indications of the level of literacy of the province of origin of the migrants supported the interpretation of aggregate level characteristics of provinces as factors in the environment affecting all persons in the area, rather than just functioning as summary measures of the distribution of characteristics of individuals in the province.

Examination of migration as assessed in 1897 supported

the study's hypotheses regarding soil fertility, literacy, and the natural rate of increase. Persons tended to travel to the great cities from relatively literate provinces that were low in soil fertility and low in natural r.

The findings for secondary industry were more complex. There was a general finding that there was some tendency for persons who were not engaged in wage work in 1897 to have disproportionately come from places with a high proportion of the population in secondary industry, even after distance to the two cities was taken into account in partial correlations or multiple regressions.

There appears no completely convincing explanation of why persons not engaged in wage work in 1897 should disproportionately come from provinces with a high proportion of the population engaged in secondary industry as compared to those who held wage work jobs in 1897. One possible explanation, which was discussed somewhat in Chapter 3, refers to a plausible model of how groups of persons decide to migrate. Most persons who lived in Moscow or St. Petersburg cities in 1897 and were not workers or servants were children, old persons, or non-working wives. Such persons would normally have travelled to the great cities in the company of a person who was a worker or servant in 1897. Perhaps the husband travelled to Moscow in the early 1890s and then in 1895 brought his wife and child to the city. Thus non-worker migration to Moscow or St. Petersburg may not have the same meaning as non-worker migration to an agricultural frontier where many "non-workers" would be farmers. Rather, non-worker migration to the great cities may indicate a certain type of migration perhaps motivated by a person seeking wage work who brings some part of his family along or else brings them to the city later.

The bringing of non-working members of one's family to

an urban industrial center may indicate a greater commitment to stay in the city for an extended period of time than if one migrated alone or in the company of other prospective workers. Bringing non-working members along may also indicate greater confidence in the possibilities for success in the urban industrial setting than would be indicated by migrating alone.

If this interpretation of the meaning of non-worker migration to Moscow and St. Petersburg is accurate, then the finding that non-worker migration is related to coming from relatively highly industrially developed places of birth is sensible in terms of the theory of migration under consideration in this research. It is possible that one effect of coming from an industrially relatively modern origin is to make a potential worker more confident about his chance of success in a major modern destination. This might be manifested in a willingness to take his family with him. Of course, this explanation is speculative and could be investigated further through archival data on the family composition of migrants.

CHAPTER 5

Migration to an Agricultural Frontier: Asiatic Russia

Asiatic Russia, the major agricultural frontier destination considered in this study, consisted of Siberia and Central Asia and did not include the Caucasus. Others have compared its settlement with the settlement of the American West, Canada, and the more remote parts of Australia (Demko 1969: 3-5; Treadgold 1957: 3-8). Migration to Asiatic Russia was a direct extension of the longterm eastward movement of the frontier of settlement in Russia. In the early fifteenth century, Russians reached the Ural Mountains (Mavor 1914: II, 211). By the mid-nineteenth century, previously sparsely settled land in the Urals and in southeastern European Russia was becoming filled. Thus the next source of free agricultural land was east of the Urals in Siberia and Central Asia (Treadgold 1957: 16). A later chapter considers migration to the areas of European Russia that were among the last to have available agricultural land, the Urals and the Donbass.

Before the emancipation of the serfs in 1861, the Tsarist government was reluctant to allow free migration to Asiatic Russia. Serfdom had never existed there, and the Tsarist government was quite concerned about the possibility that Siberia would become a haven for escaped serfs, especially if there were extensive legal migration to that area. Even within preemancipation European Russia, the relatively sparsely populated areas in southeastern Russia were known as being protective of escaped serfs (Blum 1961: 553).

By the 1880s, the overall character of migration to Asiatic Russia had changed from consisting mainly of exiles and prisoners to consisting primarily of voluntary migrants. Figure 5.1 shows the proportion of migrants to Asiatic Russia who were exiles or prisoners 1861-1914. The change in the character of migration to this area was due both to an increase in the volume of voluntary migration and to a decrease in the volume of forced migration. Table 5.1 shows the annual number of voluntary peasant migrants to Asiatic Russia 1801-1914. Many were probably illegal migrants, especially before the late 1880s. Before 1850, the volume of voluntary migration was quite small, but it increased for a time after the emancipation. In the last twenty years of the nineteenth century, the volume rose considerably and con-

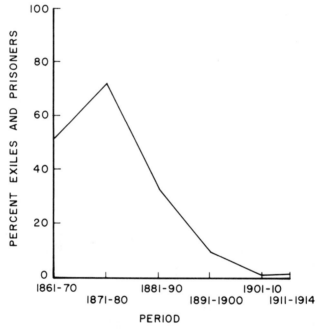

FIGURE 5.1 Percentage of Russian Migrants to Asiatic Russia who were
Exiles or Prisoners: 1861-1914

tinued rising into the early twentieth century (Treadgold 1957: 33).

Although the serfs were emancipated in the early 1860s, making serfdom as a reason for restrictions on migration to Asiatic Russia no longer valid, for bureaucratic reasons, restrictions on legal migration to Asiatic Russia were not eased until 1889 (Treadgold 1957: 24-31, 78-80).[1] One probable reason for the easing of migration restrictions in the 1880s was the increasing volume of migration before that time, as indicated in Table 5.1. Scholars have contended that the history of changes in migration policy to Asiatic Russia has been a history of legal changes that legitimated behavior that was already common (Treadgold 1957: 80; Demko 1969: 58-60).

Migrants to Asiatic Russia first settled in western Siberia. Later, as free land in western Siberia became less plentiful, settlement extended eastward into Siberia and into northern

TABLE 5.1

ANNUAL AVERAGE NUMBER OF VOLUNTARY MIGRANTS TO ASIATIC
RUSSIA: 1801-1914 (IN THOUSANDS)

Date	Annual Average Number in Thousands
1801-1850	3
1851-1860	9
1861-1870	11
1871-1880	7
1881-1890	28
1891-1900	108
1901-1910	226
1911-1914	139

[1] In 1881, a law was enacted that eased some of the earlier barriers on migration to Asiatic Russia. However, since the law was never published, it is unlikely that the 1881 legislation had much direct effect on migration to this area (Demko 1969: 58).

Central Asia (Kazakhstan), which was just south of Siberia. Researchers have often considered these two areas of settlement together as part of Siberian migration (Iamzin 1912; Treadgold 1957), although part of the destination area was not in what was legally defined as Siberia.

Table 5.2 shows the distribution of areas of destination in Asiatic Russia (Iamzin 1912).[2] Before 1896, there was very little migration to Central Asia. Even after 1896, the bulk of settlement in Central Asia was in the four northernmost provinces of Kazakhstan: Akmolinsk, Uralsk, Turgay, and Semipalitinsk.

There were some significant differences between Siberia and northern Kazakhstan as destinations. The very sparse native population of Siberia proper contrasts with the denser native population of Kazakhstan. In some Siberian areas the growing season was quite short; in Kazakhstan, the growing season was longer, but the land was quite arid in some areas (Demko 1969: 2). Even considering some agricultural difficulties in both areas, the areas of settlement by European Russians in Asiatic Russia were generally on quite good land, often of the chestnut soil variety. Most areas would be classified at soil fertility level 3 or 4 in de Tegoborskii's system (Demko 1969: 11-17).

[2] Iamzin (1912) presents data on the number of migrants stopping at migration points by province of origin in European Russia. He also presents data on the distribution of stated destinations of migrants who stopped at migration points. However, he does not present a cross-tabulation of origin by destination. Some migrants who stopped at migration points, and thus are included in Iamzin's data, stated that their destination was in the Urals, within eastern European Russia. As shown in Table 5.2, the proportion of migrants going to European Russian destinations is small: it exceeds 4 percent only in 1901-1905, when legal migration to Asiatic Russia was somewhat difficult. Since the proportion of migrants at all times who did not settle in Asiatic Russia was small (according to Iamzin's data), it is unlikely that the results are affected by the inclusion of such persons.

TABLE 5.2

DISTRIBUTION OF DESTINATIONS OF PERSONS REGISTERING AT MIGRATION
POINTS IN ASIATIC RUSSIA: 1896-1910

	1896-1900	1901-1905	1906-1910
Number of Migrants in Thousands	732	342	2,169
% Distribution of Stated Destinations of Migrants			
Western Siberia	61.5	32.8	45.7
Eastern Siberia	15.7	26.3	20.2
Northern Kazakhstan (4 provinces)	19.6	26.5	28.8
Remainder of Central Asia	.3	.3	1.6
Urals	2.1	13.8	3.7
No Answer	.9	.2	0.0
Total	100.0%	99.9%	100.0%

NOTE: Totals do not add to 100.0% due to rounding error.

QUALITY OF DATA

Two types of data are available for consideration of migration to Asiatic Russia. One type is period data on the number of migrants to Asiatic Russia in each five-year period 1885-1909, by province of origin in European Russia (Iamzin 1912). The other type of data is lifetime migration data similar to that used in the previous chapter to study migration to Moscow or St. Petersburg cities. The period migration rate for province A has as numerator the number of migrants to Asiatic Russia from province A in European Russia who registered at migration points in Asiatic Russia in a given five-year period; the denominator of the rate is the estimated population in province A at the midpoint of the five-year period, in thousands. Thus the period migration rate is a five-year, rather than an annual, rate. The lifetime migration rate has the same form as the earlier lifetime migration rates considered. For province A, the numerator is the number of persons born in province A who in 1897 lived in Asiatic Russia; the denominator of the lifetime migration rate is the number of persons, in thousands, born in province A who in 1897 lived anywhere in the Russian Empire, including province A. The province of origin is not necessarily the same as the province of birth, although they would usually be the same.

The period data are especially useful in detecting trends over time, since they identify the time at which migration occurred. The data were collected at what were called migration points in Asiatic Russia. Treadgold (1957: 90) notes that even most illegal migrants were counted at these points. Illegal migrants were not sent back to European Russia if they stopped at a migration point. In fact, even illegal migrants could obtain some help in settling from the migration point personnel (Treadgold 1957: 90). The period data and the lifetime migration data are related. The correlation of the number of lifetime migrants in Siberia or Central Asia in 1897 by province of birth in European Russia with the number of period migrants to Asiatic Russia by province of origin in European Russia 1885-1894 plus one-half the migrants 1895-1899 is .891 on the forty-one provinces of origin used in this study and .838 on all fifty provinces of European Russia. This strong relationship encourages confidence in both data sets.[3]

These data from migration points refer only to migrants to Asiatic Russia, whether or not they stayed in Asiatic Russia for any considerable period of time. There was considerable return migration. It would be possible that the number who went to Asiatic Russia from a given province was not strongly related to the number from that province who stayed in Asiatic Russia for any given period of time. If mi-

---

[3] See footnote 2, Chapter 4, for a discussion of some other data for the early nineteenth century, where a similar check on the correspondence of the results from two sources yielded results that suggested that the early nineteenth-century data examined were not of a high quality.

grants from different European Russian provinces differed considerably in their propensity to stay in Asiatic Russia once they arrived, then the interpretation of these period data would be complicated. Unfortunately, data on return migration from Asiatic Russia to individual provinces of European Russia were not located for the period studied. However, data exist on gross and net migration across the eastern border of European Russia by province of European Russia for a slightly later period.[4] The correlation between the gross and net number of migrants across this border for 1909-1914 was .995 both for the forty-one provinces of European Russia considered as origins in this study and for all fifty provinces of European Russia. These high correlations provide reason to believe that the gross migration level to Asiatic Russia by province of European Russia was strongly related to the net migration level. Thus one is fairly free to interpret the period migration data as reflecting relative differences in settlement in Asiatic Russia by province of origin in European Russia.

MIGRATION TO ASIATIC RUSSIA OVER TIME: 1885-1909

Map 5.1 shows the major routes to Siberia. Whether the destination was Kazakhstan or more northerly Siberia proper, the route was identical for much of the journey (Demko 1969: 96-97). Both streams generally travelled

---

[4] The number of gross migrants from province A to province B in a given time period is the number of persons in that time period who migrated from province A to province B. The number of net migrants from province A to province B in a time period is the number of migrants from province A to province B in the time period minus the number of migrants from province B to province A in that time period. The source of the data on the number of migrants in each direction across the border of Asiatic Russia is Russia, Tzentral'nyi Statisticheskii Komitet (1915).

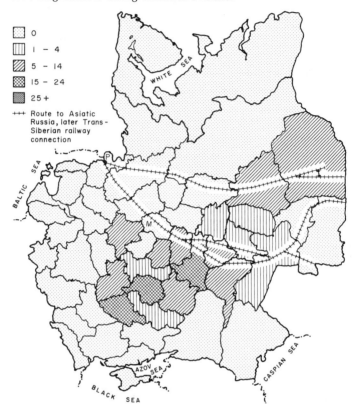

MAP 5.1 Period Migration Rate to Asiatic Russia: 1890-1894

through European Russia to Omsk. Those destined for
Kazakhstan then turned south, often to settle in Akmolinsk
province (Demko 1969: 96-103). Since streams to both
Siberia and Central Asia travelled through Omsk, the research will employ the natural logarithm of the distance to
Omsk in hundreds of miles as the distance measure. Other
distance measures such as the natural logarithm of the distance to the Asiatic Russian border or the natural logarithm
of the distance to Tomsk were also investigated. These dif-

ferences in the distance measure made very little difference in the results.

The Trans-Siberian Railway was laid along the route shown in Map 5.1. The first leg of the railway was finished in 1896 (Treadgold 1957: 11). This railway greatly facilitated migration to Asiatic Russia. Fares were charged per unit of distance travelled, but they were subsidized for legal migrants (Treadgold 1957: 31).

A social institution that also facilitated migration to Asiatic Russia was the scout. A scout was a person employed by a village or a part of a village that was contemplating migration to Asiatic Russia. He would travel to Asiatic Russia, assess conditions, and sometimes contract for land for the group to settle on. He would then return to report his findings to his employers (Demko 1969: 59-60; Treadgold 1957: 95, 121). This social institution greatly reduced problems of information concerning a distant place from which return would be difficult. After 1904, the Tsarist government required the use of scouts for legal migration to Asiatic Russia (Treadgold 1957: 129), although this regulation was not always observed (Demko 1969: 88-89).

Although there was some mining in Siberia, persons generally travelled to Asiatic Russia to farm on fairly abundant land in a setting where personal freedom was more available than in European Russia. Recalling Table 2.8, it is clear that Asiatic Russia had a more frontier type of occupational environment than did European Russia. Both sexes performed less nonagricultural activity in Asiatic Russia than in European Russia, while at the same time, persons of both sexes were somewhat more involved in mining.

The model of migration predicts that migrants to Asiatic Russia would tend to come from areas of high soil fertility, low literacy, little secondary industry, and high rates of natural increase. Many of these expectations are not new to this study. Variously conceived, population pressure has often been cited as a major cause of migration to Asiatic Russia (Demko 1969; Treadgold 1957).

Although such impressions are probably accurate, researchers have rarely subjected them to systematic investigation. The most relevant study of the effect of population pressure on migration to Asiatic Russia was Demko's investigation of Russian migration to Kazakhstan. Demko (1969: 67-74) regressed the number of estimated migrants by province of birth in European Russia (estimated from the 1926 Soviet Census) on the population of the European Russian province of birth and the distance of the province from Kazakhstan. He found that distance and the population of the province of birth together explained 70 percent of the variance in the number of migrants to Kazakhstan by province of birth. However, he observed that the black earth (high soil fertility) provinces had more migrants to Kazakhstan than would be expected from their distance from Kazakhstan and the population in the European Russian province. He also observed that the provinces in the European Russian industrial center had fewer migrants than would be predicted on this basis. Although Treadgold's and Demko's earlier studies have been quite helpful in understanding the nature of migration to Asiatic Russia, it is hoped that this study can contribute to a more detailed understanding of migration to Asiatic Russia as well as provide a partial test of the general model of migration under examination.

The research predicts that over time migrants to Asiatic Russia will change from more "pioneering" to more "mass" in Petersen's (1958) terms. This would mean that migrants would increasingly come from less literate, higher soil fertility origins, with a higher rate of natural increase and less of the population engaged in secondary industrial work. Migrants who went to Asiatic Russia were choosing not to migrate to modern, urban destinations in European Russia. This study contends that eventually persons migrated to Asiatic Russia due to the relative inadequacy of available land at their origin rather than due to a general spirit of adventure. Thus, moving to Asiatic Russia was more modern behavior than staying in one's province of birth, but it was less modern than migrating to a major urban destination in European Russia.

Maps 5.1 and 5.2 show the period migration rates for 1890-1894 and 1905-1909. By the early 1900s, migration to

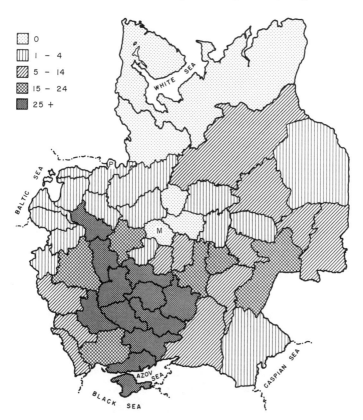

MAP 5.2 Period Migration Rate to Asiatic Russia: 1905-1909

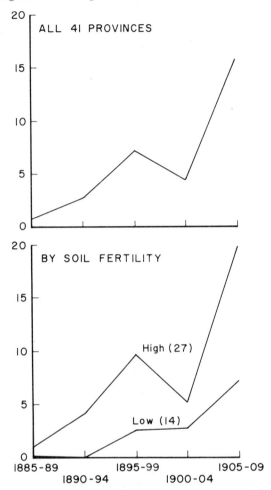

FIGURE 5.2 Period Migration Rates to Asiatic Russia 1885-1909 by Level of Soil Fertility

Asiatic Russia had become concentrated in the south central, high soil fertility area of European Russia.

Figure 5.2 shows migration rates to Asiatic Russia over time for all forty-one provinces and separately according to the level of soil fertility. It is apparent that rates generally increased over time except for a sharp dip between 1900-1904. Three factors probably contributed to the decrease in migration to Asiatic Russia during that period: a famine in 1901-1902, the Russo-Japanese War in 1904, and the Revolution of 1905. The famine in 1901-1902 was less severe than the famine in 1891-1892 (Florinsky 1953: II, 1159, 1167). However, the lower volume of migration at the earlier time and the legal change easing migration in 1889 may have caused the 1891-1892 famine to have had less effect on migration than the milder food shortage in 1901-1902. The 1901-1902 famine was more severe in the southern than in the northern part of European Russia. During the Russo-Japanese War, it became more difficult to be a legal migrant (Demko 1969: 88), as the Tsarist government wanted to utilize all available space on the Trans-Siberian Railway to ship military supplies and personnel to the front. Thus the major effect of the restriction on legal migration was most likely the effective increase of railway ticket costs to migrants. As early as 1904, the general social disruption associated with the Revolution of 1905 also may have decreased migration to Asiatic Russia. The effects of the Revolution of 1905 were also more severe in southern than in northern European Russia. It will be seen in Figure 5.3 that the dip in migration in 1901-1904 actually extended through 1905.

The bottom panel of Figure 5.2 clearly indicates that the higher soil fertility area entirely accounts for the decrease in migration 1900-1904. Although the restriction on legal migration leading to higher railway costs should have affected migrants regardless of their origin, the observed difference suggests the greater importance of the famine in 1901-1902 and the Revolution of 1905. However, if the Russo-Japanese War had not occurred, the rate of migration to Asiatic Russia from the lower soil fertility area might have increased considerably in 1900-1904, rather than remaining practically unchanged.

Figure 5.3 shows the annual number of migrants to Asiatic Russia 1887-1909. The dips in 1901-1902 and in 1904-1905 are clear. The earlier dips coincide with the famine, while the later dips coincide with the Russo-Japanese War and the Revolution of 1905. Table 5.3 indicates the proportion of migrants to Asiatic Russia who were

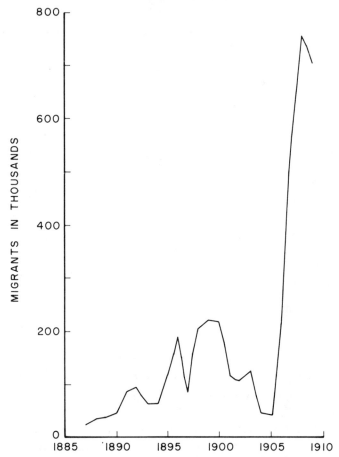

FIGURE 5.3 Annual Number of Migrants to Asiatic Russia: 1887-1909

legal migrants 1896-1909 (Treadgold 1957: 34). The effects of the tightening of legal migration during the Russo-Japanese War are also clear here.

Looking again at Figure 5.2, the gap in the rate of migration between the higher soil fertility provinces and the lower soil fertility provinces widened generally over time, with the higher soil fertility area always having the higher rate. This trend may indicate that as information about Asiatic Russia became more common, persons from the less modernized, more agricultural areas increasingly decided to migrate to this area. In contrast, at an earlier time, general attitudes toward risk taking associated with literacy may have played a more important role in the decision to migrate to Asiatic Russia.

Table 5.4 indicates the change in the type of areas from

TABLE 5.3

PERCENTAGE OF MIGRANTS TO ASIATIC RUSSIA WHO WERE
LEGAL MIGRANTS: 1896-1909

Year	% Legal
1896	62
1897	61
1898	60
1899	54
1900	70
1901	67
1902	65
1903	67
1904	18
1905	7
1906	49
1907	80
1908	52
1909	52

TABLE 5.4

CORRELATIONS BETWEEN PERIOD MIGRATION RATES TO ASIATIC RUSSIA 1885-1909
AND LIFETIME MIGRATION RATES TO MOSCOW OR ST. PETERSBURG CITIES 1897 AND
LIFETIME MIGRATION RATES TO ASIATIC RUSSIA 1897 (ON 41 PROVINCES)

	1885-89	1890-94	1895-99	1900-04	1905-09
Lifetime Migration Rate to Moscow or St. Petersburg 1897	-.183	-.277	-.298	-.334	-.390
Lifetime Migration Rate to Asiatic Russia 1897	.474	.849	.769	.250	.414

NOTE: p< .05 for underlined coefficients, two-tailed tests.

which migrants to Asiatic Russia came, as compared to migrants to Moscow and St. Petersburg. This table shows correlations between migration rates over time and lifetime migration to Asiatic Russia (both sexes combined) and with lifetime migration to Moscow and St. Petersburg. It is clear that over time, the pattern of origins of migrants to Asiatic Russia became increasingly dissimilar from the pattern of origins of migrants to the two great cities. This trend is consistent with the interpretation that at first migrants tended to come from areas that induced in their residents a general propensity toward migration, while, over time, factors other than a general willingness to take risks became more important.

Note also in Table 5.4 the relatively low correlations between period and lifetime migration to Asiatic Russia. This is the case even though, as mentioned earlier, the volume of migration before 1897 implied by the period data by province of origin in European Russia agreed well with the implied volume of lifetime migration in 1897 to Asiatic Russia by province of birth in European Russia. These low correlations suggest that interpretation of lifetime migration to Asiatic Russia in 1897 as representing the pattern of migration in any particular period may be risky. In order to understand migration to Asiatic Russia, it is necessary to consider both the period and the lifetime migration data.

Data on the individual characteristics of migrants to Asiatic Russia over time also reflect the changing composition of the migration stream. Table 5.5 shows the average amount of money brought by a sample of migrant families prior to 1896 and up to 1903 (Iamzin 1912). The average amount of money brought declined over time. However, it is clear that this decrease in monetary assets was due almost

TABLE 5.5

AVERAGE AMOUNT OF MONEY BROUGHT BY MIGRANT FAMILIES TO ASIATIC RUSSIA

Date	Average Number of Rubles per Family	Percentage of Families with more than 150 Rubles	Average Number of Rubles per Family Excluding those with more than 150 Rubles	n
To 1896	94	13	76	2969
1897-1899	85	11	70	2095
1900-1901	79	7	71	1833
1902	71	4	72	697
1903	30	0	31	447

TABLE 5.6

ALLOTMENTS OF MIGRANT FAMILIES PREVIOUS TO MIGRATION FROM EUROPEAN RUSSIA, AS COLLECTED AT CHELIABINSK

Date	Median Holding in Dessiatines	% Landless	% with at least 6 Dessiatines	n
1894	1-2	14	16	1244
1895	1-2	16	16	13706
1896	2-3	19	18	28631
1898	2-3	15	25	23238
1899	3-4	11	33	28783
1900	2-3	17	21	24654
1901	2-3	17	22	13107
1902	2-3	13	26	12230
1903	2-3	21	29	10844
1906	1-2	27	19	21997

entirely to a decrease over time in the proportion of migrant families who brought a large amount of money (over 150 rubles). The data in Table 5.5 suggest the interpretation that over time the proportion of persons who were fairly well-off decreased but that the proportion of destitute persons coming to Asiatic Russia did not increase.

Table 5.6 shows the average size of holding of migrant families in European Russia previous to migration. These data were collected at one of the major migration points, Cheliabinsk. Contrary to the evidence in Table 5.5, there was not an appreciable decline in the average holding in European Russia over time. Nor was there a noticeable decline in the proportion of migrants who had large holdings in European Russia (Iamzin 1912). Treadgold cautions that interpreting economic position from size of allotment is very misleading because soil quality varies enormously in European Russia and also because sources of income other than those derived from the land were common in many parts of European Russia. This study agrees with the contention that reliance on amount of land held can be very misleading.

Table 5.7 indicates the correlations between explanatory variables and period migration rates to Asiatic Russia. Even from the beginning, migrants tended to come from provinces with a fairly high level of soil fertility. However, Table 5.7 also shows the auxiliary occupation variable—the proportion of those mainly engaged in agriculture who also had an auxiliary occupation. The relationship of migration to auxiliary occupation became progressively more negative. This means that over time, persons increasingly tended to come from provinces where a large proportion of the population had no source of economic support other than traditional agriculture. Migrants also tended to come from less literate provinces. The increasingly negative correla-

TABLE 5.7

CORRELATIONS OF EXPLANATORY VARIABLES WITH MIGRATION RATES TO ASIATIC
RUSSIA OVER TIME: 1895-1909 (ON 41 PROVINCES)

	1885-89	1890-94	1895-99	1900-04	1905-09
Soil	.300	.569	.484	.242	.425
Agri w/aux	-.081	-.161	-.331	-.386	-.394
Lit7483	-.166	-.275	-.344	-.378	-.430
WorkSec97	-.106	-.168	-.225	-.263	-.281
Nat r8185	-.211	-.036	.158	.464	.472
Nat r8690	.036	.037	.242	.458	.518
Nat r9195	-.100	-.260	-.052	.531	.396
Nat r9600	.002	.175	.274	.459	.575
Nat r0105	.267	.404	.409	.326	.542
lnDistAsRus	-.059	-.187	-.035	.307	.238
Mean	.808	2.794	7.161	4.302	15.544
s.d.	2.513	4.708	8.416	5.297	15.592

NOTE: $p < .05$ for underlined coefficients, two-tailed tests.

tions with the secondary industry variable also provide
some evidence that migrants increasingly came from less
industrially modern provinces, although the coefficient for
the secondary industry variable never becomes statistically
significant.

The most interesting observation from Table 5.7 is that
the provinces of origin of migrants to Asiatic Russia increasingly were those with a high rate of natural increase.
This is consistent with the expectation that population pressure would increasingly become a factor in migration to
Asiatic Russia and that an agricultural frontier may be the
type of destination to consider if one expects to find migration as an outlet for population pressure. If, in Davis's
(1963) terms, migration is used as a "multiphasic demographic response," then such an agricultural frontier desti-

nation may make migration appear as a realistic alternative to persons who might be reluctant to migrate to an urban, industrial destination. Recall that natural r was not important for out-migration generally nor for migration to Moscow or St. Petersburg cities.

In Table 5.7, one can examine the relation of natural r to period migration to Asiatic Russia in either of two ways. On the one hand, the changing correlation of natural r for a given time period, such as 1881-1885, with migration rates over time can be examined. On the other hand, one can say that the relevant time to consider natural r relative to migration in a given time period is immediately before the time period of migration. With this second strategy, one would consider natural r 1881-1885 in relation to migration 1885-1889, natural r 1886-1890 for migration 1890-1894, and so on. Whichever strategy is adopted, the interpretation is the same: natural r, the indicator of population pressure, obtains an increasingly positive correlation with migration to Asiatic Russia with time.

Another interesting, but puzzling, observation from Table 5.7 is the changing relationship of migration to distance. Usually migration rates are negatively related to any measure of distance between the origin and the destination. The distance measure employed for migration to Asiatic Russia is the natural logarithm of the distance to Omsk in hundreds of miles. However, when other distance measures were used, such as the logarithm of the distance to Tomsk or the logarithm of the distance to the border of Asiatic Russia, the same pattern of increasingly positive correlations with distance over time was found.[5]

[5] Kursk province was a somewhat extreme outlier for the period migration rates to Asiatic Russia for the early periods. This province had a much higher rate of migration to Asiatic Russia than would be expected on the basis of all provinces. When Kursk was excluded from the analysis, the pattern of an increasingly positive correlation over time be-

The changing relation of distance to migration is perhaps explicable in light of the increasing importance of scouts. It may be that the information obtained from scouts greatly reduced the actual and perceived risks of migration and thus might be expected to minimize the effects of distance on migration propensity. However, there is still no reason to expect a positive relation with distance. It is not reasonable that it was actually an *advantage* to start from a long distance from Asiatic Russia. However, the positive relation with distance is not due to the spurious relation with distance of some socio-economic variable considered in this study. In Table 5.8, the standardized stepwise and non-stepwise multiple regression coefficients are shown. Even when the other explanatory variables considered are entered simultaneously with distance, distance eventually attains a significantly positive relation with migration rates, as does natural r. Although it is possible that if other explanatory variables had been considered, a normal negative relation of migration rates to distance might have persisted over time, examination of a rather large range of potential explanatory variables did not affect the increasingly positive relation of these migration rates to distance.[6]

---

tween migration rates and both distance and natural r persisted. Thus Kursk was left in the set of provinces of origin considered for migration to Asiatic Russia.

[6] In Table 2.10, it is clear that the correlation between the natural logarithm of distance to Asiatic Russia and natural r 1881-1885 is somewhat weaker than the correlation between the distance measure and natural r for some other time periods. It was important to determine whether the eventually positive relation of distance to migration rates over time was due in part to the relatively weak relationship between the distance measure and natural r 1881-1885. Regressions were also computed for period migration to Asiatic Russia by using natural r 1886-1900 as the population pressure variable and by alternatively using population density 1897 or the population growth rate 1885-1897 as the indicator of the level of population pressure at the origin. The increasingly positive rela-

TABLE 5.8

STANDARDIZED MULTIPLE REGRESSION COEFFICIENTS FOR PERIOD MIGRATION TO
ASIATIC RUSSIA: 1885-1909
(ON 41 PROVINCES)

	1885-1889	1890-1894	1895-1899	1900-1904	1905-1909
Stepwise Regressions					
Soil	.434	.670	.484		.350
	(7.838)	(24.336)	(11.919)		(6.204)
Lit					
Work					
Nat r	-.369	-.280		.467	.347
	(5.659)	(4.235)		(12.042)	(6.204)
Distance				.310	.301
				(5.323)	(5.265)
R^2	.208	.391	.234	.312	.384
F	4.988	12.209	11.919	8.615	7.703
Non-Stepwise Regressions					
Soil	.316	.645	.470	.100	.353
	(2.647)	(14.096)	(5.860)	(.356)	(4.026)
Lit	-.247	.025	-.034	-.088	.019
	(.773)	(.010)	(.110)	(.110)	(.005)
Work	-.071	-.156	-.111	-.002	-.044
	(.117)	(.726)	(.289)	(.000)	(.050)
Nat r	-.511	-.321	-.080	.371	.340
	(7.358)	(3.705)	(.179)	(4.373)	(3.962)
Distance	-.004	-.088	.040	.331	.298
	(.001)	(.446)	(.073)	(5.532)	(4.867)
R^2	.251	.414	.250	.334	.386
F	2.350	4.944	2.334	3.510	4.393

NOTE: $p < .05$ for underlined coefficients. F ratios in parentheses.

A substantive argument can be made as to why the
relation of migration to distance might become positive, although this argument is only intended as a *possible* explanation of the positive relation with distance and was not
considered before the finding about distance was obtained.

---

tion of migration rates with distance over time persisted, although the
coefficient of distance did not always become statistically significantly
positive.

If Maps 5.1 and 5.2 are examined, it is clear that the center of migration to Asiatic Russia shifted westward over time. This was a general shift to the more agricultural area in the central southwestern part of European Russia that was not the result simply of a concentration of migration within the Ukraine. That it was not just a shift to the Ukraine can be seen by examining Map 2.1. The area of heavy migration in 1905-1909 does not correspond to the Ukraine by either definition of the Ukraine presented in Chapter 2. It is possible that at first distance operated in the usual manner. Persons who, for whatever reasons, were inclined to migrate to Asiatic Russia did so, with those more distant from Asiatic Russia being less likely to migrate. One can imagine that in any given province, there were some people who were inclined to migrate to Asiatic Russia and others who had no such inclination. The supply of people inclined to migrate to Asiatic Russia may have become "exhausted" at an earlier date in provinces closer to Asiatic Russia than in provinces that were more distant from this area. Thus the center of migration to Asiatic Russia shifted westward over time, somewhat like ripples in a pond emanating out from a stone that struck the pond's surface. Admittedly this explanation is ad hoc and speculative. To determine whether this type of explanation has any general validity, one would have to examine migration over time to other destinations, preferably frontier destinations, where migration to such a destination had a fairly well-defined beginning and could be examined from this beginning.

The extent to which distance was an impediment to migration certainly should have lessened after the first leg of the Trans-Siberian Railway was opened in 1896. Figure 5.3 shows that there was a jump in the volume of migration to Asiatic Russia in 1896, although there was a large dip in 1897. However, the effect of the eased transportation offered by the railway should have been to generally increase migration rates from all parts of European Russia. There is no reason why it should have caused migration rates to cease to be negatively related to distance, since fare was still charged in accordance to the distance travelled.

Table 5.9 shows the correlations between various explanatory variables and period migration rates by the level of soil fertility of provinces, with provinces at soil fertility levels 1-2 combined into the low soil fertility group

TABLE 5.9

CORRELATIONS BETWEEN EXPLANATORY VARIABLES AND PERIOD MIGRATION RATES
TO ASIATIC RUSSIA, BY LEVEL OF SOIL FERTILITY: 1885-1909

	1885-89	1890-94	1895-99	1900-04	1905-09
Low Soil Fertility (Levels 1-2), 14 provinces					
Soil	.360	.481	.451	.351	.432
Agri w/aux	-.391	-.650	-.576	-.602	-.494
Lit7483	-.393	-.547	-.559	-.553	-.427
WorkSec97	-.186	-.151	-.278	-.282	-.275
Nat r8185	.479	.451	.500	.511	.454
lnDistAsRus	.359	.409	.500	.491	.424
Mean	.100	.015	2.521	2.685	7.053
s.d.	.288	.025	4.158	5.147	10.635
High Soil Fertility (Levels 3-5), 27 provinces					
Soil	.280	.500	2.82	.014	.112
Agri w/aux	.140	.247	.050	-.075	-.078
Lit7483	-.049	-.012	.020	-.120	-.137
WorkSec97	-.078	-.067	-.064	-.189	-.189
Nat r8185	-.399	-.294	-.099	.385	.351
lnDistAsRus	-.053	-.176	-.061	.306	.279
Mean	1.175	4.236	9.567	5.140	19.947
s.d.	3.044	5.271	9.096	5.271	16.078

NOTE: p< .05 for underlined coefficients, two-tailed tests.

and provinces with soil fertility at levels 3-5 combined into a high soil fertility group. The number of provinces in each group is quite small. Thus results from Table 5.9 must generally be regarded as suggestive rather than conclusive. Correlations with the proportion of those in agriculture with an auxiliary occupation are shown, since there is little chance for substantial variability in soil fertility when it can assume only two or three different values. Also, as argued in Chapter 2, the major difference in soil fertility seemed to be between the high and the low soil fertility group, as defined in Table. 5.9.

A somewhat different pattern of change over time is suggested in the two soil fertility areas. In the low soil fertility area, migrants tended to come disproportionately from the less literate provinces within the low soil fertility area after 1885-1889. In the high soil fertility area, the major change was an increasingly positive general relationship with natural r over time. These differences in patterns are also found in regressions performed separately in the two soil fertility areas (not shown). The average level of natural r was lower in the low soil fertility area than in the high soil fertility area. In the low soil fertility area, the mean of natural r 1881-1885 was twelve per thousand population, while in the high soil fertility area the mean was fifteen per thousand population. Thus, in general, the level of population pressure was greater in the higher than in the lower soil fertility area. However, the relation of natural r within the low soil fertility area is positive and fairly strong at all times. It is also interesting that in the low soil fertility area, where the holding of an auxiliary occupation by a person in agriculture was fairly common, the relation of the proportion holding such an auxiliary occupation with migration rates was generally negative. That is, within the low soil fertility area, those provinces where a greater proportion of those in agriculture had no other means of economic support had relatively higher migration rates to Asiatic Russia than did other low soil fertility provinces.

It seems that several hypotheses about migration to Asiatic Russia are consistent with the data in Table 5.9, although these differ according to the two soil fertility areas. The hypothesis about decreasing importance of literacy is supported by the results for the low soil fertility area, while the expectation about natural r is supported in the higher soil fertility area. More detailed data would be necessary to further disentangle the interrelations between changes in migration to Asiatic Russia.

LIFETIME MIGRATION TO ASIATIC RUSSIA

Lifetime migration rates to Asiatic Russia in 1897 can be computed as were similar rates for migration to Moscow and St. Petersburg. Correlations between the explanatory variables and the lifetime migration rates and among the lifetime migration rates are shown in Table 5.10. All groups tended to come from provinces that were high in soil fertility. Also, all groups tended to come from relatively close to Asiatic Russia. Map 5.3 shows the lifetime migration variable for females. The geographic pattern in Map 5.3 can be seen as a kind of averaging of the patterns in Maps 5.1 and 5.2. The female lifetime migration rate is closely related to the other lifetime migration rates, as shown in Table 5.10. As was the case for general out-migration, if one considers the rates by sex and work status in 1897, the correlations within work groups are higher than within sex groups. For instance, the correlation of the rates for male and female non-workers is .991, while the correlation between female workers and non-workers is only .666. This agreement within work groups is not surprising, since many of the

TABLE 5.10

CORRELATIONS AND PARTIAL CORRELATIONS FOR LIFETIME MIGRATION
TO ASIATIC RUSSIA: 1897 (ON 41 PROVINCES)

	M	F	MW	FW	MNW	FNW
Correlations with Explanatory Variables						
Soil	.530	.499	.410	.407	.530	.497
Lit7483	-.289	-.305	-.377	-.363	-.276	-.300
WorkSec97	-.153	-.201	-.240	-.250	-.151	-.197
Nat r8185	.023	.079	.171	.180	.019	.077
lnDistAsRus	-.450	-.416	-.796	-.823	-.359	-.395
Correlations Among Migration Rates						
M	1.000	.990	.609	.708	.990	.988
F		1.000	.569	.688	.989	.999
MW			1.000	.949	.499	.546
FW				1.000	.620	.666
MNW					1.000	.991
FNW						1.000
Partial Correlations Controlling for Distance Measure						
Soil	.484	.446	.374	.391	.396	.287
Lit7483	-.283	-.300	-.537	-.562	-.355	-.310
WorkSec97	-.194	-.245	-.460	-.533	-.294	-.285
Nat r8185	-.039	.032	.153	.181	.294	.295
Mean	15.278	10.823	31.241	15.121	13.780	10.743
s.d.	.572	11.289	10.184	22.702	11.209	10.235

NOTE: p<.05 for underlined coefficients, two-tailed tests.

male and female non-workers were in families who migrated to Asiatic Russia in order to farm.

The significant negative correlations of the lifetime migration rates with distance lend some support to the explanation of the changing relation of distance to the period migration rates with time. However, the correlation between

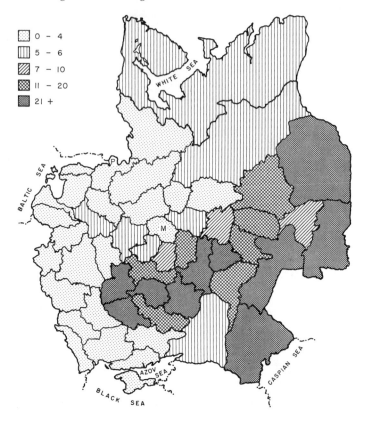

MAP 5.3 Female Lifetime Migration Rate to Asiatic Russia: 1897

distance and the period migration rates did not become positive until the 1900-1904 period—after 1897. Even so, the observation that the negative correlations between the lifetime migration rates and the distance measure are stronger than even the negative correlations between the period migration rates through 1895-1899 and the distance measure still give some slight support to the notion that an area may become depleted of persons wishing to migrate to a particular destination.

Since the correlations between the distance measure and the lifetime migration rates are all negative, it makes some sense to consider partial correlations where the effect of distance is controlled. These partial correlations are also shown in Table 5.10. The relations with soil fertility remain positive and are significant for all groups except female non-workers. There is some strengthening of the negative relations with literacy and the secondary industry variable also. In the regressions (not shown), a similar pattern appears. Soil fertility is positively related to migration rates (also significantly for female non-workers in the regressions), and literacy is significantly negatively related to migration rates for workers when included with distance in the stepwise regressions.

LIFETIME MIGRATION TO ASIATIC RUSSIA COMPARED TO GENERAL OUT-MIGRATION

The chance that a person migrated to Asiatic Russia, given that he migrated out of his province of birth at all, can also be considered. This is the conditional probability that a person lived in Asiatic Russia if he did not live in his European Russian province of birth in 1897. A similar conditional probability was considered in Chapter 4 for migration to Moscow and St. Petersburg. This conditional rate has as numerator the number of persons born in province A who in 1897 lived in Asiatic Russia; the denominator is the number of persons in thousands who were born in province A and in 1897 lived in the Russian Empire but not in province A. Thus the denominator is the number of out-migrants from province A.

In Chapter 3, the characteristics of origins of out-migrants were investigated. It was clear that out-migrants were not randomly selected from provinces. They tended, for instance, to come disproportionately from highly literate provinces. The correlations between this allocational migration variable to Asiatic Russia and explanatory variables are shown in Table 5.11. Partial correlations on the natural logarithm of distance to Omsk in hundreds of miles are also shown. The pattern is generally similar to that in Table 5.10 for migration to Asiatic Russia not confined to comparison with out-migrants. However, as was the case for migration to Moscow and St. Petersburg, the relationships are generally somewhat stronger when only out-migrants are considered as the comparison group than when the general population by province of birth, whether migrant or not, is the group for comparison.

All of the correlations between explanatory variables other than soil fertility and the allocational migration rates are stronger than the correlations between explanatory vari-

TABLE 5.11

CORRELATIONS AND PARTIAL CORRELATIONS FOR LIFETIME MIGRATION TO ASIATIC RUSSIA
PER THOUSAND MIGRANTS OUT OF THE PROVINCE OF BIRTH: 1897 (ON 41 PROVINCES)

	M	F	MW	FW	MNW	FNW
Correlations						
Soil	.451	.403	.295	.328	.441	.377
Lit7483	-.418	-.361	-.393	-.368	-.365	-.334
WorkSec97	-.288	-.254	-.231	-.228	-.274	-.248
Nat r8185	.229	.175	.403	.273	.137	.143
lnDistAsRus	-.606	-.632	-.605	-.789	-.538	-.614
Partial Correlations Controlling for Distance Measure						
Soil	.443	.387	.244	.319	.420	.350
Lit7483	-.500	-.439	-.469	-.556	-.412	-.397
WorkSec97	-.402	-.370	-.329	-.436	-.358	-.354
Nat r8185	.281	.219	.499	.434	.157	.175
Mean	126.745	127.686	100.000	60.658	142.025	138.735
s.d.	83.091	103.100	82.358	65.552	90.843	106.555

ables other than soil fertility and the simple migration rates. The stronger relations with the allocational variables suggest that migration may not have been a two-stage process in which a person first decided he wanted to migrate *somewhere* and then chose the particular destination. If migration were such a two-stage process, then migrants to a particular destination should be more similar to out-migrants generally than to all persons whether or not they were migrants. In terms of this study, if migration were a two-stage process, then the origins of migrants to a particular destination, such as Asiatic Russia, would be more similar to the origins of migrants generally than to the origins of all persons. However, since there is some evidence that migration to Asiatic Russia was not a two-stage process, this evidence suggests that migrants to Asiatic Russia were responding to particular circumstances and attractions of Asiatic Russia rather than acting in response to a general urge to migrate.

In the partial correlations, the relations between the literacy and industry variables are stronger with the allocational migration rates than with the simple migration rates for all groups except workers. Literacy was the most important variable for migration to the destination at the other end of the modernity scale from Asiatic Russia: Moscow and St. Petersburg cities. It is possible that persons who were attracted to Asiatic Russia were from places that led them not only to have little desire to migrate to a modern, urban destination, such as Moscow or St. Petersburg, but were also from areas where persons actively did not want to migrate to places such as the two great cities.

Persons who migrated to Asiatic Russia may have not migrated *anywhere* if no agricultural frontier had been available. If this interpretation is accurate, and if destinations with free agricultural land are the only types of destinations that can effectively function as outlets for population pressure in agricultural areas of origin, then it seems unlikely that population pressure can motivate migration in those cases in which no destination with unsettled agricultural land is available. The differences between simple and allocational migration rates to Asiatic Russia and to Moscow and St. Petersburg will be discussed further in Chapter 8.

CONCLUSIONS

The examination of migration to Asiatic Russia led to both substantial and methodological results. The changing pattern of origins of migrants over time illustrated the manner in which a population may respond to the opening of a new frontier for settlement. The increasing tendency of migrants to come from provinces with a high rate of natural increase was interpreted as an indication of the increasing appeal of an agricultural frontier as a possible migration destination to victims of population pressure. However, the great change in the pattern of migration before 1897 also shows that simple interpretation of the lifetime migration rates computed from the 1897 census could be misleading without the additional information from the period data. This is an illustration of the fact that it is dangerous to interpret cross-sectional lifetime migration data as representing migration patterns during any given period if there is no reason to believe that the pattern of migration has remained fairly stable for some time.

Evidence was presented that suggested that the decision to migrate to Asiatic Russia was not the result of a two-stage process wherein persons first decided to migrate and then chose Asiatic Russia as a destination. In Chapter 4, evidence was presented that supported the existence of such a two-stage migration process for migration to Moscow or St. Petersburg cities. Since the mechanism of the migration decision-making process may differ according to the potential destination, researchers and policy makers should be careful not to view migrants as an undifferentiated group or they may be led astray in their planning by this unwarranted assumption.

CHAPTER 6

Migration to Destinations of Intermediate Modernity

This chapter considers migration to destinations whose modernity is intermediate between that of the great cities of Moscow and St. Petersburg and the agricultural frontier in Asiatic Russia. The destinations considered are the provinces with intensive mining activity in the Urals and the Donbass and the provinces of European Russia excluding Moscow and St. Petersburg cities and the provinces in the Urals and Donbass just referred to. These remaining European Russian provinces are considered together as a group.[1]

These two groups of provinces, the mining provinces, and the remainder of European Russia were intermediate in modernity both culturally and industrially between the extreme types of destinations considered earlier in Chapters 4 and 5. Table 2.8 shows that the occupational distribution in each group for each sex was intermediate both in terms of the proportion of each sex who were workers or servants and in terms of the occupational distribution of the workers and servants. For both males and females, a higher proportion of worker-servants were workers in secondary industry

[1] The three Baltic provinces and Moscow and St. Petersburg provinces outside of the capital cities of Moscow and St. Petersburg are included in the destinations considered. Kovno province had considerable migration to the Baltic provinces. Overall, though, the results are only slightly affected when the Baltic provinces are excluded from consideration as destinations. There also seemed no reason to exclude the hinterlands of Moscow and St. Petersburg provinces from the destinations, since for destinations, it is quite easy to distinguish between Moscow and St. Petersburg cities and the rest of the provinces in which they are located.

in the remainder of European Russia than in the Urals-Donbass provinces. For females, the occupational distribution in the remainder of European Russia is clearly more modern than in the Urals-Donbass provinces. However, considering mining along with secondary industry makes the Urals-Don more modern in occupational distribution of males than the rest of European Russia.

The two areas were also intermediate in literacy. Table 6.1 shows the proportion literate in the various detailed des-

TABLE 6.1

PERCENTAGE LITERATE IN DETAILED DESTINATIONS: 1897

	% Literate
Moscow and St. Petersburg Cities	57
European Russia other than Moscow and St. Petersburg Cities and the Urals-Donbass	25
Urals-Donbass	21
European Population in Asiatic Russia	∿16

tinations considered (Rashin 1956: 298, 308; Russia 1915). From the percentages literate, the rest of European Russia appears more culturally modern than the group of Urals-Donbass provinces.

In this chapter the two areas will be considered separately and then compared. However, many of the results for these destinations of intermediate modernity only become interesting when compared with the results for the two great cities and Asiatic Russia. That comparison occurs in Chapter 8.

As stated in Chapter 1, when this study began there was no expectation about the characteristics of origins of migrants to destinations of intermediate modernity. However, the research revealed that migrants whose destinations were in European Russia but not in Moscow or St. Petersburg had origins that were intermediate in modernity between the origins of migrants to Siberia and the origins of migrants to Moscow or St. Petersburg (Anderson 1974). This finding created interest in considering additional intermediate destinations. Two such destinations were defined by dividing European Russia without Moscow and St. Petersburg cities into the Urals-Don provinces and the remainder of the provinces of European Russia. From Tables 2.8 and 6.1, the rest of European Russia seems somewhat more modern than the Urals-Don area. The research will reveal whether this difference is reflected in the characteristics of origins of migrants to the two destinations of intermediate modernity.

MIGRATION TO THE URALS OR DONBASS

This section considers migration to those provinces of European Russia that were the major centers of mining. These same provinces included some of the last fertile, previously uncultivated land to be settled in European Russia. By 1897, however, virtually no arable land remained unsettled in these provinces.

For the purposes of this study, Perm and Orenburg provinces are included in the Urals. The research considers Don and Ekaterinoslav provinces to be included in the Donbass. Often Ufa and Vyatka provinces are also included in the Urals, while Kharkov is often considered to be in the Donbass. Table 6.2 shows that the four provinces included in the Urals-Donbass in this study included the vast majority of male mining workers in European Russia. Also, in each of the included provinces, the proportion of male worker-servants in mining is higher than in any of the excluded provinces (Russia 1905b).

The Urals and Donbass areas differed in their mining histories. The Urals became a mining center long before the Donbass. Mining in the former area began in the early

TABLE 6.2

THE ROLE OF THE URALS-DONBASS IN MINING IN THE RUSSIAN EMPIRE: 1897

	Males in Mining in Thousands	% of Male Worker- Servants in Mining
Russian Empire	196	3
European Russia	138	3
Don Province	20	14
Ekaterinoslav Province	26	19
Perm Province	53	29
Orenburg Province	13	18
Four Chosen Urals-Donbass Provinces Together	111	21
Vyatka Province	6	8
Ufa Province	5	8
Kharkov Province	0	0
Three Urals-Donbass Provinces not Chosen Together	11	5
Siberia	30	10

eighteenth century, and by the mid-eighteenth century over half of the iron mined in the Urals was exported. Largely due to the production in the Urals, Russia was the world's largest pig-iron producer in 1800 (Blum 1961: 294-295). Before the emancipation of the serfs, much of the labor in the mines was performed by possessional serfs who were owned by the mines. These serfs tended to live with their families in villages near the mines. Often the sons of possessional serf miners also became possessional serf miners. Thus even before emancipation, a hereditary labor force had grown up in mining in the Urals. The Donbass area did not begin substantial mining activity until the 1870s, at which point the industry was heavily financed by foreign capital. In the 1890s, the Donbass mining operation was in full production (Crisp 1976: 154), while by 1897, the Urals was in a decline.

The nature of agricultural conditions also differed in the two areas. Land in the Donbass was of better quality, and previously unsettled land was available there later than it was in the Urals. As late as the 1850s, the government encouraged settlement in the Donbass (Blum 1961: 559, 614).

Mining may be less modern activity than other types of industrial enterprise. Social scientists normally group extractive mining with farming, fishing, and forestry in the category of primary industry. In the Urals and Donbass, 77 percent of the males in the census classifications "mining" or "smelting" were in "mining" (Russia 1905b). Thus even those persons in the Urals-Don area engaged in the mining industry were heavily concentrated in the extractive rather than the processing part of the industry. This study considers industrial activity in mining more modern than subsistence agriculture or work as an agricultural laborer but less modern than work in secondary industry.

Maps 6.1 and 6.2 show male worker and non-worker migration rates to the Urals-Donbass, respectively. The construction of the rates is similar to that of those in earlier chapters. For the non-worker rate for province A, the numerator is the number of non-workers born in province A who in 1897 lived in the Urals-Donbass provinces; the denominator is the number of non-workers in thousands who were born in province A and in 1897 lived anywhere in the Russian Empire. The maps show that migration was heavy near the Donbass and the Urals areas. Migration was also relatively heavier from the higher than from the lower soil fertility area.

Table 6.3 shows the correlations between the explanatory variables and the migration rates. The distance measure used is the natural logarithm of the distance in hundreds of

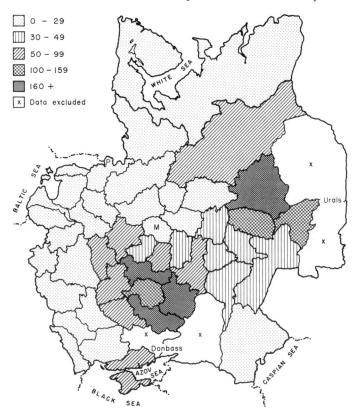

MAP 6.1   Male Worker Lifetime Migration Rate to the Urals or Donbass:
1897

miles to the closer of the Urals or Donbass. For all groups,
correlations with soil fertility are positive and significant,
and with the distance measure they are negative and significant. The impression received from the maps that migration was heavy close to the destinations and that it was relatively heavy in the higher soil fertility area is thus supported. Correlations with literacy are negative for all
groups, significantly so for workers. Most of the significant

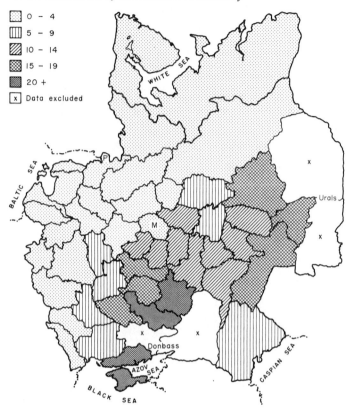

MAP 6.2 Male Non-Worker Lifetime Migration Rate to the Urals or Donbass: 1897

relationships disappear when distance is taken into account in the partial correlations at the bottom of Table 6.3. Only the positive relation with soil fertility remains for non-workers and for females as a group. The positive relation with soil fertility for non-workers is consistent with the interpretation that non-worker migrants were often agricultural settlers at an earlier time. The positive relation with soil fertility is similar to what was found in Chapter 5 for

TABLE 6.3

CORRELATIONS AND PARTIAL CORRELATIONS FOR MIGRATION TO THE
URALS OR DONBASS: 1897 (ON 41 PROVINCES)

	M	F	MW	FW	MNW	FNW
Correlations						
Soil	.566	.572	.479	.508	.580	.569
Lit7483	-.267	-.295	-.349	-.367	-.256	-.287
WorkSec97	-.083	-.131	-.222	-.209	-.041	-.119
Nat r8185	.161	.300	.138	-.227	.255	.310
lnDistU-D	-.678	-.650	-.565	-.534	-.699	-.654
Partial Correlations Controlling for Distance Measure						
Soil	.300	.324	.237	.294	.317	.317
Lit7483	-.098	-.144	-.312	-.261	-.196	-.133
WorkSec97	-.157	-.213	-.269	-.300	-.058	-.199
Nat r8185	-.032	.169	.123	.080	.292	.183
Mean	12.709	9.106	51.637	26.269	8.816	8.571
s.d.	11.056	8.876	54.363	31.889	7.765	8.321

NOTE: $p < .05$ for underlined coefficients.

migration to Asiatic Russia. The regressions had essentially the same results as the partial correlations and thus are not shown here.

Migration to the Urals and Donbass was examined in order to determine which factors were related to the choice of destination between these two areas. For this purpose, an allocational migration variable similar to that in Chapter 4 for allocation of migrants between Moscow and St. Petersburg was constructed. The variable is the conditional probability that a migrant goes to the Donbass given that he migrates to either the Donbass or the Urals. The rate for province A has as numerator the number of persons born in province A who in 1897 lived in the Donbass; the denominator is the number of persons in thousands who were born in province A and in 1897 lived in either the Donbass or the Urals. An allocational distance variable was also created, which was the percentage by which the Urals were closer than the Donbass. This variable is analogous to the distance variable for the allocation of migrants between Moscow and St. Petersburg. When the migration variable was related to the study's normal explanatory variables and the allocational distance variable, the only variable that had a significant relationship to migration either in the correlations or the regressions was the distance variable. Thus, within the universe of explanatory variables considered in this study, despite the historical and climatic differences between the Urals and the Donbass, the only factor that appeared important in determining which destination was chosen was the relative distance to the two potential destinations. This finding supported the consideration of the Urals and the Donbass together as one destination; it also halted further investigation of the differences between the Urals and the Donbass for the purposes of this study.

MIGRATION WITHIN EUROPEAN RUSSIA BUT NOT TO MOSCOW OR ST. PETERSBURG CITIES OR THE URALS-DONBASS PROVINCES

Maps 2.9 and 2.10 show the distribution of migrants within European Russia by province of destination. The destinations other than Moscow and St. Petersburg provinces formed a kind of semicircle around the lower half of European Russia. Maps 6.3 and 6.4 show the male worker and non-worker migration rates to destinations in European Russia other than Moscow or St. Petersburg cities and other than the Urals-Donbass provinces considered earlier in this chapter. Worker migration was heavy from the central area near Moscow.

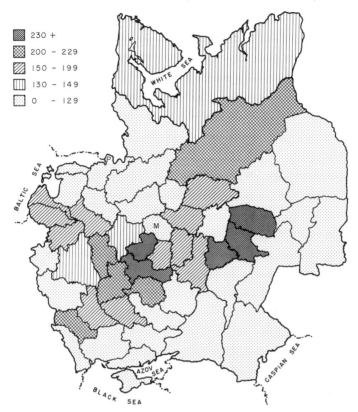

▨	230 +
▨	200 - 229
▨	150 - 199
▥	130 - 149
▦	0 - 129

MAP 6.3 Male Worker Lifetime Migration Rate in European Russia other than to Moscow, St. Petersburg, Urals or Donbass: 1897

Table 6.4 shows the correlations between the explanatory variables and the migration rates to the remainder of European Russia. Non-workers tended to come from provinces with a low rate of natural increase.

Perhaps migrants who chose European Russian destinations other than the two great cities or the Urals-Donbass did so because their provinces of birth were fairly distant from the more popular destinations. To investigate this pos-

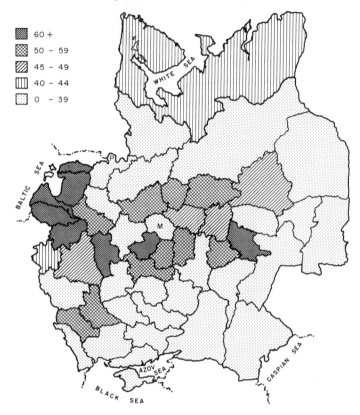

MAP 6.4 Male Non-Worker Lifetime Migration Rate in European Russia other than to Moscow, St. Petersburg, Urals or Donbass: 1897

sibility, a distance variable that was the natural logarithm of the distance in hundreds of miles to the closer of Moscow City, St. Petersburg City, the Urals or the Donbass (lnDist-MPDU in Table 6.4) was created. If minor destinations were chosen because the named major destinations were distant, then this new distance variable should have a posi-

TABLE 6.4

CORRELATIONS FOR MIGRATION WITHIN EUROPEAN RUSSIA NOT TO
MOSCOW, ST. PETERSBURG, THE URALS OR THE DONBASS: 1897 (ON 41 PROVINCES)

	M	F	MW	FW	MNW	FNW
Soil	-.066	.090	.154	.323	-.097	.110
Lit7483	.246	.117	-.098	-.163	.248	.092
WorkSec97	.333	.157	-.015	-.074	.271	.126
Nat r8185	-.381	-.252	-.196	-.092	-.322	-.226
lnDistMStP	-.516	-.421	-.288	-.196	-.405	-.395
lnDistMPDU	.257	.196	.218	.184	.281	.185
Mean	53.992	37.972	146.008	116.809	146.007	32.425
s.d.	18.643	12.391	65.273	47.907	12.938	11.302

tive correlation with migration rates. Although the correlations are positive, none of them are statistically significant. The natural logarithm of the distance to the closer of Moscow or St. Petersburg cities (lnDistMStP) also appears in Table 6.4. The correlation with the measure of distance to the two great cities is negatively related to the migration rates, significantly for all groups except workers. This negative relationship means that migration rates to the remainder of European Russia were higher the closer the province of birth was to either Moscow or St. Petersburg cities. This finding is consistent with the notion that attitudes favorable to migration may have diffused from the two great cities. The possibility of diffusion of attitudes favoring migration from the cities was mentioned in Chapter 4. However, in that chapter no test of this idea could be made since the destinations considered were Moscow and St. Petersburg cities, the supposed centers for diffusion of innovation. The positive correlations with lnDistMPDU were insignificant, and the correlations with lnDistMStP were negative and often significant. Thus it seemed unwarranted to use a distance measure as a control in partial correlations. In Stepwise regressions, lnDistMPDU was also never statistically significant for any group.

CONCLUSIONS

Comparing Tables 6.3 and 6.4, migrants to the Urals-Donbass tended to come from somewhat higher soil fertility and somewhat less literate provinces than migrants to the remainder of European Russia. Thus in terms of the types of destinations considered in this research, the origins of migrants to the remainder of European Russia were generally somewhat more like the origins of migrants to Moscow or St. Petersburg cities, while the origins of migrants to the Urals-Don were somewhat more like the origins of migrants to Asiatic Russia.

Most correlations for both intermediate destinations are statistically insignificant. This would be the case if the relations of origins of migrants to destinations of intermediate modernity had characteristics that were intermediate between the characteristics of origin of migrants to more modern and the characteristics of origin of migrants to less modern destinations.

In the next chapter, the characteristics of origin of migrants to two other cities in European Russia are considered: Odessa and Kiev. These cities played a special role for Jews and reflect the fact that although normal socio-economic variables can explain much about migration, there are situations in which non-socio-economic, cultural variables are important. In such cases, restricting one's attention only to socio-economic variables can be misleading. In the final chapter, the patterns of migration to the major destinations considered in Chapters 3 through 6 are compared for a general test of the proposed model of migration.

CHAPTER 7

Modern Destinations in the Pale: Migration to Odessa and Kiev

Odessa was the third largest city in European Russia in 1897, and Kiev was the fifth largest. Chapter 4 demonstrated that Odessa differed considerably from the two larger European Russian cities in the structure of the labor force for each sex. In the course of this research, determinants of migration to Odessa were investigated. The original purpose of the investigation was to determine how similar the migration pattern to Odessa was to the migration pattern to Moscow or St. Petersburg. It was expected that the migration pattern to a city would not simply be determined by the size of the city: the heavy concentration of Odessa's labor force in commercial and semicommercial activity, such as day labor on the docks, might affect outsiders' perception of the modernity of Odessa or the perception of the permeability of her labor market. Because development of commerce often occurs historically before substantial development of industry, commercial development may occur without substantial other social changes that typically accompany modernization. Thus, even though Odessa was a young city, founded in 1794, its commercial emphasis still may have affected its real or perceived modernity.

Investigation of the determinants of migration to Odessa using the socio-economic explanatory variables employed in the rest of the research showed that the only factor that was important for migration to Odessa was the natural logarithm of distance from Odessa (Anderson 1974: 318-331). In a personal communication, Patricia Herlihy suggested that Odessa may have been a modern destination for

Jews. In 1897, most Jews were required to live in a set of provinces in western European Russia called the Pale of settlement. The eastern boundary of the Pale is shown in Map 7.1. Only Jews with a high level of education or in certain specialized occupations were legally allowed to live outside of the Pale. Map 7.1 also shows the percentage of each province's population that was Jewish. It is clear that the bulk of Jewish settlement was contained within the Pale. (Mavor 1914: II, 207). As neither Moscow nor St. Peters-

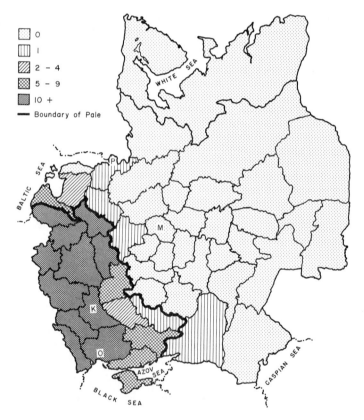

MAP 7.1 Percentage Jewish: 1897

burg were in the Pale, Odessa may have been the most modern destination available for Jewish potential migrants.

The purpose of this chapter is the investigation of the effects of restrictive migration and settlement legislation referring to a particular ethnic group on the migration of that ethnic group. As discussed in Chapter 5, legislation does not always seem to determine people's behavior. Because the results of this chapter are not intended to be directly comparable with the results of the other chapters, and as no other chapter has focussed in detail on ethnic characteristics of provinces, there seemed no reason to exclude the provinces in the Urals and the Donbass from the list of origins considered. However, the three Baltic provinces are excluded from this list as they are still quite different from the rest of European Russia, within or outside of the Pale. Similarly, Moscow and St. Petersburg provinces are excluded since their inclusion would make it unlikely that Odessa or Kiev could even appear as regional centers. Kherson province, in which Odessa is located, and Kiev province are also excluded from the list as they contain the destinations of interest. This leaves forty-three provinces of origin. If the Urals and Donbass provinces had also been excluded, there would be only thirty-nine provinces of origin. The results considering the thirty-nine provinces of origin rather than the forty-three provinces of origin are quite similar. At times, statistical significance is obtained with forty-three provinces, when it is not so obtained with thirty-nine provinces.

Map 7.2 shows the lifetime migration rate to Odessa for females. Rates decrease rapidly with distance from Odessa. However, they tend to be higher from a province in the Pale than from a province removed from Odessa by a similar distance but not in the Pale. Comparing Maps 7.1 and 7.2 shows that migration to Odessa was concentrated within that part of the Pale with the heavier Jewish settlement.

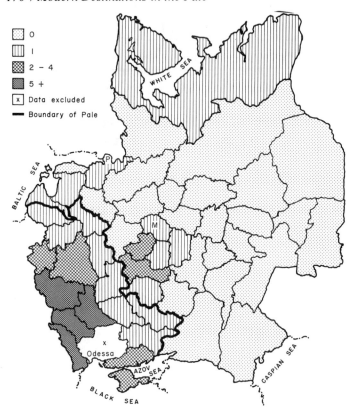

MAP 7.2 Female Lifetime Migration Rate to Odessa: 1897

Kiev was the next largest city in the Pale after Odessa. Migration to this city was examined in order to determine whether it was a modern destination for Jews. Kiev's population was considerably more literate than that of Odessa, with the former's population showing 44 percent literate in 1874 and the latter's showing only 31 percent literate in 1873 (Rashin 1956: 296-297). Thus, Kiev's literacy level would seem to make it as likely or a more likely candidate for a modern destination for Jews than Odessa. Map 7.3

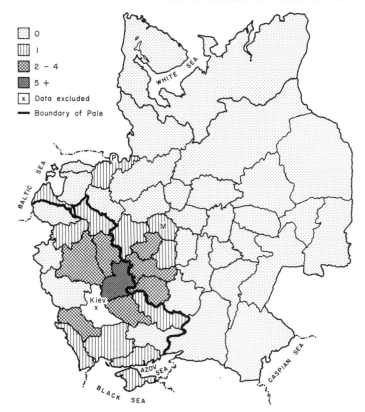

MAP 7.3 Female Lifetime Migration Rate to Kiev: 1897

shows the female lifetime migration rate to Kiev. This rate does not appear as closely related either to the boundaries of the Pale or to the proportion Jewish in a province's population as was the female migration rate to Odessa.

The impression that Jewish settlement in areas of origin differentially affected migration to Odessa as compared to migration to Kiev is supported by the correlations of explanatory variables with migration rates to the two cities shown in Table 7.1. For each city, the distance measure

TABLE 7.1

CORRELATIONS AND PARTIAL CORRELATIONS FOR MIGRATION TO ODESSA
AND KIEV: 1897 (ON 43 PROVINCES)

	Odessa		Kiev	
	M	F	M	F
Correlations				
Soil	.286	.278	.214	.150
Lit7483	-.224	-.260	-.183	-.135
WorkSec97	-.095	-.129	-.119	-.105
Nat r8185	.185	.198	.063	.107
%Jewish	.535	.591	.206	.282
Pale	.512	.545	.270	.340
Dist	-.730	-.769	-.578	-.607
Partial Correlations Controlling on Distance Measure				
Soil				
Lit7483	.095	-.031	-.031	.045
WorkSec97	.015	-.032	-.047	-.024
Nat r8185	-.204	-.221	-.127	-.086
%Jewish	.249	.333	-.234	-.155
Pale	.138	.170	-.129	-.057
Mean	1.767	1.106	1.257	.808
s.d.	1.917	1.717	1.812	1.279

NOTE: p< .05 for underlined coefficients, two-tailed tests.

employed is the natural logarithm of the distance to the city in hundreds of miles. In Table 7.1, "Pale" is a variable that has the value zero if a province is not in the Pale and the value one if the province is in the Pale. Thus a positive correlation between a migration rate and the "Pale" variable means that migration rates tend to be higher from provinces in the Pale than from provinces not in the Pale.

For each city, distance is significantly related to migration rates. Rates decline with increasing distance between the origin and the destination. However, both the percentage Jewish in the province of birth and the location of the province of birth in the Pale are significantly positively related to migration propensity to Odessa but not to Kiev.

For both Odessa and Kiev, the migration rates are lifetime rates similar to those in earlier chapters. For Kiev, for instance, the rate for province A has as numerator the number of persons born in province A who in 1897 lived in Kiev City; the denominator of the rate is the number of persons born in province A who in 1897 lived anywhere in the Russian Empire, including province A and Kiev. Migration data were available separately by work status in 1897 for Odessa but not for Kiev. Since the purpose of this chapter is to compare Odessa with Kiev, only data referring to total sex groups are presented.

The partial correlations at the bottom of Table 7.1 show that even when the distance measures are controlled for, migration to Odessa remains positively related to the percentage Jewish, significantly so for females. For migration to Kiev, the coefficients for percentage Jewish and the location of the province in the Pale remain insignificant and also become negative.

Restricting the analysis to those provinces within the Pale indicates that the correlations for migration to Odessa with percentage Jewish remain positive (.298 for males and .327 for females). Restricting attention to the Pale, the correlations for migration to Kiev with percentage Jewish remain negative ($-$ .211 for males and $-$ .235 for females). All of the correlations that consider only provinces of birth within the Pale are statistically insignificant, partially because there are only fifteen provinces in the Pale. For these correlations concentrating on the Pale, the only province excluded was the one in which the destination city was located. With fourteen cases, a correlation of a magnitude of at least .497 is necessary for significance at the .05 level.

What might explain the difference in the propensity of persons from provinces of heavy Jewish settlement to migrate to Odessa as compared to Kiev? Three factors seem possible explanations. First, Kiev, along with certain other cities within the Pale, was forbidden to Jews as a place of permanent settlement (Mavor 1914: II, 207). Most Jews were allowed to live in Kiev for a legal maximum of six months at a time, and the only Jews legally allowed to settle permanently in Kiev were certain "privileged" Jews with advanced degrees or in certain special occupations (Dubnow 1975: III, 19-20). Second, whether this settlement rule was enforced or not, the existence of such a rule may have discouraged Jews from desiring to go to Kiev.[1] Jewish set-

---

[1] Different definitions of "urban" were often used for different purposes (Fedor 1975). Although Jews were legally barred from living in rural areas, according to the 1897 Census, in all provinces in which a substantial number of Jews lived, more lived in areas defined as "rural" than in areas defined as "urban." It is unlikely that this large number of Jews were in violation of the law. What is more likely is that a different definition of "urban" was used for determining where Jews were allowed to live than was used in the census definition. Vital registration data in the nineteenth century also made it clear that different definitions of "urban" were used for different administrative purposes. For a discussion of these differences see Coale, Anderson, and Härm (1979).

It is possible that the definition of the boundaries of Kiev City differed in its application to where Jews were allowed to live from the definition of the boundaries of Kiev City for the purposes of the 1897 Imperial Russian Census. Jews were forbidden to live in rural areas in 1882-1883 (Fedor 1975: 100). Many of the Jewish migrants to Odessa may have been persons who were forced to leave rural areas due to the legal change. However, even if this were the case, the difference in migration patterns from areas of heavy settlement between Odessa and Kiev is still interesting, and the interpretation in this study is not affected.

tlement in Odessa was subjected to no similar restrictions. Third, Kiev's status as a center of anti-Semitism may also have discouraged settlement by Jews (Dubnow 1975: III, 19-20) or by persons from areas of heavy Jewish settlement.

In 1897, 13 percent of Kiev City's population was recorded as Jewish; only 12 percent of the population of all of Kiev province was Jewish. Since the proportion Jewish in the city (where Jewish settlement was supposedly illegal) was greater than the proportion Jewish in the province as a whole (where although there were restrictions on Jewish settlement in rural areas, Jews were free to live in towns and other cities), it does not seem that the restriction on Jewish settlement in Kiev City was strictly enforced. The other two factors may have been quite important.

As the mean values of the migration rates in Table 7.1 indicate, overall migration rates were higher to Odessa than to Kiev. Both the percentage of a province that was Jewish and the location of the province inside or outside of the Pale were positively correlated with migration rates to Odessa and insignificantly or negatively correlated with migration to Kiev. This shows that provinces with a large proportion of Jews in their population tended to exhibit higher migration rates to Odessa than did other provinces that had a lower proportion of Jews in their population.

There are two possible explanations for this finding. On the one hand, Jewish migrants may have favored Odessa as a destination to a greater extent than did non-Jews. On the other hand, persons who were born in a province with a large proportion of Jews in the population may have tended to choose Odessa rather than Kiev as a destination, whether or not the actual migrants were Jewish. From the available data there is no way to determine which of these two possible explanations is correct. However, the first explanation seems the more likely of the two. Examination of nineteenth-century internal passports in the Soviet archives might help to resolve this question.

Table 7.2 shows the stepwise regression results obtained by entering all of the explanatory variables used consistently in this study along with the percentage Jewish in a

TABLE 7.2

STANDARDIZED STEPWISE REGRESSION COEFFICIENTS FOR MIGRATION
TO ODESSA AND KIEV: 1897 (ON 43 PROVINCES)

	Odessa		Kiev	
	M	F	M	F
%Jewish	.243 (4.303)	.283 (6.996)		
Nat r8185	-.150 (1.783)			
Dist	-.672 (29.016)	-.631 (34.850)	-.578 (20.553)	-.607 (23.949)
R^2	.593	.652	.334	.369
F	18.927	27.529	20.593	23.949

NOTE: p< .05 for underlined coefficients. F ratios in parentheses.

province and the variable indicating whether a province is in the Pale. For migration to Kiev, the distance measure is the only variable that is statistically significant at any stage. For female migration to Odessa, when both the distance measure and the percentage Jewish in a province are entered, both coefficients are statistically significant, and migration rates are positively related to the percentage Jewish in the province of birth. For male migration to Odessa, when the distance measure and the percentage Jewish are both entered, the percentage Jewish variable barely misses statistical significance. Percentage Jewish has an F ratio of 3.95, when an F ratio of 4.08 would be required for statistical significance at the .05 level. However, when natural r 1881-1885 is also entered into the regression, the coefficient for percentage Jewish remains positive and becomes statistically significant. No other variables are statistically significant at any point in the stepwise regressions for migration to Odessa. When natural r 1881-1885 is entered along with the distance measure and the percentage Jewish for female migration to Odessa, percentage Jewish retains its statistical significance.

Examination of migration to Odessa and Kiev leads to observations about both the effects of legislation and of cultural characteristics of places. Discounting lying to census takers, Jews did tend to reside in the Pale as required by law, and it appears that Kiev's restrictive settlement rules along with its anti-Semitic reputation may indeed have discouraged Jews from migrating to that city. For Asiatic Russia, on the other hand, there was evidence that, aside from the initial legislation opening Asiatic Russia to legal settlement in the 1880s, successive legislative changes seemed to be of little consequence. The conditions under which legislation does or does not affect behavior are difficult to characterize.

The proportion of a population that is Jewish is a cultural rather than a socio-economic characteristic of that province. When general social theories are tested in particular historical settings, it is often tempting for the researcher to disregard cultural characteristics of the society that are particular to the given time and place. The importance of concentration of Jewish settlement in the province of birth for migration to Odessa illustrates that researchers must be careful to consider whatever particular historical and cultural factors are important in the setting in which the researcher has chosen to test his model. As is the case with the effect of legislation, the conditions under which cultural characteristics are generally important are for the most part unknown. Only future research that takes account of both socio-economic and cultural variables can clarify the interrelations between these two types of factors.

CHAPTER 8

Conclusions: Comparison of Migration
Patterns to Detailed Destinations

In Chapters 4 through 6, migration patterns to various destinations in the Russian Empire were examined. Some of the results in those chapters are interesting in themselves. However, other results are only meaningful in comparison with the results of the analysis of migration to other destinations. In this chapter, the results of the analysis of migration patterns to various destinations are compared. Also, the performance of this study's migration model is evaluated by summarizing the extent of confirmation or refutation of the hypotheses stated in Chapter 1.

The detailed destinations considered in this study can be ranked in order of decreasing modernity: Moscow and St. Petersburg cities, European Russia other than the great cities and other than the Urals-Donbass provinces, the Urals-Donbass provinces, and Asiatic Russia. In Table 8.1, the correlations among the migration rates to these four destinations are presented according to sex and work status in 1897.

Residents of a given province, call it province A, may prefer a migration destination to have a certain level of modernity. If so, persons from province A will tend to migrate to destinations with that preferred modernity level. Migrants from province A who do not choose a destination at the preferred modernity level may be more likely to choose a destination with a modernity level close to the level of the generally preferred destination than to choose a destination with a modernity level that is quite dissimilar from the modernity level of the generally preferred destination. Similarly, provinces may differ in their average preferred modernity level of destinations. If there exists a reluctance by residents of a given province to move to destinations at a modernity level very dissimilar from the modernity level of the generally preferred destination, then the correlations in Table 8.1 should show a very regular pattern. The more dissimilar two destinations are in modernity—the further they are separated in the table—the more negative should be the correlation between the migration rates to those two destinations. For instance, a province with a relatively high migration rate to Moscow and St.

TABLE 8.1

CORRELATIONS AMONG MIGRATION RATES TO DETAILED DESTINATIONS:
1897 (ON 41 PROVINCES)

	Male				Female			
	M-StP	ER-MSUD	U-D	AsRus	M-StP	ER-MSUD	U-D	AsRus
Total								
M-StP	1.000	.316	-.280	-.301	1.000	.193	-.373	-.351
ER-MSUD		1.000	-.114	-.005		1.000	-.282	-.063
U-D			1.000	.625			1.000	.567
AsRus				1.000				1.000
Workers								
M-StP	1.000	-.056	-.343	-.426	1.000	-.056	-.355	-.373
ER-MSUD		1.000	.041	.075		1.000	.034	-.316
U-D			1.000	.401			1.000	.121
AsRus				1.000				1.000
Non-Workers								
M-StP	1.000	.309	-.272	-.270	1.000	.155	-.381	-.356
ER-MSUD		1.000	-.286	-.147		1.000	-.211	-.063
U-D			1.000	.597			1.000	.555
AsRus				1.000				1.000

NOTE: p< .05 for underlined coefficients, two-tailed tests.

Petersburg cities (the most modern destination) should have a moderate migration rate to the remainder of European Russia (the second most modern destination), a lower migration rate to the Urals-Donbass provinces (the third most modern destination), and an even lower migration rate to Asiatic Russia (the least modern destination).

Generally in Table 8.1 there is a pattern of stronger negative correlations (or weaker positive correlations) between migration rates to various destinations the greater the destinations differ in modernity. Thus the results are consistent with the model of destination preference according to province of origin just outlined. The pattern is followed perfectly for female workers and for the total male group. The regularity of the pattern of stronger negative correlations the more dissimilar in modernity two destinations are is broken only by a reversal for some groups in the position of Asiatic Russia and the position of the Urals-Donbass.

This research considers Asiatic Russia a less modern destination than the Urals-Donbass provinces. Recall that the Urals-Donbass contained some of the last arable, unsettled land in European Russia. In Chapter 5, it was shown that over time the period migration rate to Asiatic Russia became increasingly negatively correlated with the migration rate to the two great cities. In 1897, some of the non-worker migrants in the Urals-Don provinces would have been persons who were agricultural settlers at an earlier date. Period data on migration to the Urals-Don by province of origin would be interesting to examine to determine whether migration had the same changing pattern over time in that area as in Asiatic Russia. Perhaps if the Imperial Russian Census had been taken in 1910 rather than in 1897, the reversals of Asiatic Russia and the Urals-Donbass found in Table 8.1 would not have occurred.

This research expects that relatively modern origins will

tend to send migrants to more modern destinations more often than will less modern origins. If such were the case, then a pattern of intercorrelations of migration rates, such as shown in Table 8.1, could result from the preferred modernity level of destination held by residents of province A being determined by the relative modernity of province A. Figure 1.1 schematically represented the expected change in the relation of migration rates to destinations in terms of the modernity of the destination and the socio-economic characteristics of the province of origin. Industrially or culturally modern origins are expected to have higher migration rates to modern destinations than will less culturally or industrially modern origins. Provinces with a high level of population pressure and where traditional agriculture is very important are expected to have relatively high migration rates to less modern destinations.

Tables 8.2 and 8.3 show the correlations and partial correlations between the explanatory variables consistently used in this study and migration rates to the various destinations. Distance measures were included primarily as statistical controls. Thus the correlations with the distance measures are not shown in Table 8.2. Chapter 6 showed that there was no reasonable distance measure to use as a statistical control for migration to the remainder of European Russia. Thus the remainder of European Russia does not appear as a destination in Table 8.3.

The pattern of correlations and partial correlations is generally quite consistent with the expectations of this research, as schematically represented in Figure 1.1. Generally, the literacy of provinces of birth assumes an increasingly negative correlation with migration rates the less modern the destination. Industrial development of the province of birth has, as expected, a similar relationship with migration rates to that of literacy, although the pattern for secondary indus-

TABLE 8.2

CORRELATIONS FOR COMPARISON OF DETAILED DESTINATIONS: 1897 (ON 41 PROVINCES)

	Male				Female			
	M-StP	ER-MSUD	U-D	AsRus	M-StP	ER-MSUD	U-D	AsRus
Total								
Soil	-.535	-.066	.566	.530	-.639	.090	.572	.499
Lit7483	.846	.246	-.267	-.289	.800	.117	-.295	-305
WorkSec97	.480	.333	-.083	-.153	.420	.157	-.131	-.201
Nat r8185	-.528	-.381	.161	.023	-.541	-.252	.300	.079
Workers								
Soil	-.658	.154	.479	.410	-.612	.323	.508	.407
Lit7483	.700	-.098	-.349	-.377	.619	-.163	-.367	-.363
WorkSec97	.236	.015	-.222	-.240	.182	-.074	-.209	-.250
Nat r8185	-.506	-.196	.138	.171	-.482	-.092	-.227	.180
Non-Workers								
Soil	-.496	-.097	.580	.530	-.646	.110	.569	.497
Lit7483	.863	.248	-.256	-.276	.843	.092	-.287	-.300
WorkSec97	.591	.271	-.041	-.151	.524	.126	-.119	-.197
Nat r8185	-.522	-.322	.255	.019	-.563	-.226	.310	.077

NOTE: p< .05 for underlined coefficients, two-tailed tests.

try is somewhat weaker than the pattern for literacy. Soil fertility of the origin has a generally negative relation with the modernity of the destination. The least modern destinations, Asiatic Russia and the Urals-Donbass provinces, have the strongest positive relationships with soil fertility, while the correlation between soil fertility and migration rates to the rest of European Russia are close to zero, and the relations with migration to the two great cities are strong and negative.

In Tables 8.2 and 8.3, natural r never attains a significant positive relation with migration rates to any destination, with the single exception of the correlation for female

TABLE 8.3

PARTIAL CORRELATIONS FOR MIGRATION RATES TO DETAILED DESTINATIONS:
1897 (ON 41 PROVINCES)

	Male			Female		
	M-StP	U-D	AsRus	M-StP	U-D	AsRus
Total						
Soil	-.411	.300	.484	-.597	.324	.446
Lit7483	.766	-.098	-.283	.687	-.144	-.300
WorkSec97	.259	-.157	-.194	.133	-.213	-.245
Nat r8185	-.185	-.032	-.039	-.166	.169	.032
Workers						
Soil	-.610	.237	.374	-.554	.294	.391
Lit7483	.500	-.312	-.537	.338	-.261	-.562
WorkSec97	-.153	-.269	-.460	-.304	-.300	-.533
Nat r8185	-.132	.123	.153	-.042	.080	.181
Non-Workers						
Soil	-.360	.317	.396	-.594	.317	.287
Lit7483	.790	-.196	-.355	.784	-.133	-.310
WorkSec97	.449	-.058	-.294	.325	-.199	-.285
Nat r8185	-.240	.292	.294	-.230	.183	.295

NOTE: p< .05 for underlined coefficients, two-tailed tests.
Coefficients are partialled on the appropriate distance measure.

non-workers. However, the pattern of an increasingly positive relation with migration rates the less modern the destination is maintained. The negative or insignificant relations between natural r and migration rates to the more modern destinations counters the argument that population pressure is a positive determinant of migration to modern destinations. In the total research, a strong positive relation between migration rates and natural r, the indicator of population pressure, was found only for period migration to Asiatic Russia in the later time periods studied. The positive relation between natural r and migration rates to the Urals-

Donbass provinces for non-workers suggests that a similar pattern to that for Asiatic Russia in the later time periods may have obtained for the Urals-Donbass toward the end of the agricultural settlement era in that region. In Tables 8.2 and 8.3, as in Table 8.1, the only exceptions to the proposed pattern of relations are some reversals between Asiatic Russia and the Urals-Donbass provinces. As discussed in Chapter 5, when migration patterns have changed in the recent past, the interpretation of lifetime migration measured at one point in time may be misleading.

Table 8.4 presents standardized regressions for all four destinations by sex and work status in 1897. The results for the rest of European Russia are not completely comparable to the other results, however, because four rather than five explanatory variables are included in the analysis for the rest of European Russia as a destination. Also, as indicated by the F ratio for the total equation, the regressions are not statistically significant as a whole for the rest of European Russia. When the regression as a whole does not attain a statistically significant F ratio, the interpretation of the coefficients in this regression may be especially misleading; when the results of the regressions for migration to the rest of European Russia are ignored, literacy and soil fertility vary in sign and magnitude across the various destinations in a manner similar to that in Tables 8.2 and 8.3, and the pattern obtained is generally quite regular. The results for secondary industry and natural r are not consistent with the proposed model. There are two possible reasons for this divergence from the model's predictions, other than that the model might be incorrect. First, the correlations among the explanatory variables may have affected the regression coefficients, as discussed in Chapter 4. Second, the negative relation between migration to Asiatic Russia and natural r may be due to the changing nature of migration to Asiatic Russia over time, as mentioned several times previously.

TABLE 8.4

STANDARDIZED REGRESSIONS FOR COMPARISON OF DETAILED DESTINATIONS: 1897
(ON 41 PROVINCES)

	Male				Female			
	M-StP	ER-MSDU	U-D	AsRus	M-StP	ER-MSDU	U-D	AsRus
Total								
Soil	.053	.048	.327	.492	-.156	.227	.366	.448
	(.38)	(.06)	(3.59)	(8.12)	(3.58)	(1.22)	(4.36)	(7.59)
Lit7483	.898	-.163	.162	-.054	.630	.017	.298	-.014
	(49.32)	(.325)	(.530)	(.051)	(27.56)	(.00)	(1.73)	(.00)
WorkSec97	-.237	.298	-.169	-.106	-.238	.083	-.206	-.161
	(6.34)	(2.01)	(1.00)	(.37)	(7.09)	(.13)	(1.44)	(.75)
Nat r8185	.179	-.376	-.081	-.238	.136	-.289	.131	-.163
	(3.85)	(3.83)	(.29)	(2.19)	(2.46)	(2.08)	(.73)	(.92)
Dist	-.446		-.569	-.372	-.545		-.503	-.348
	(26.42)		(14.68)	(8.53)	(43.68)		(11.16)	(6.71)
R^2	.920	.199	.528	.455	.862	.108	.515	.392
F	38.78	2.24	7.84	5.83	43.61	1.10	7.43	4.52
Workers								
Soil	-.234	.106	.090	.126	-.226	.352	.233	.146
	(6.76)	(.276)	(.168)	(1.41)	(6.72)	(3.12)	(1.40)	(2.06)
Lit7483	.588	-.386	-.205	-.255	.454	-.125	.002	-.181
	(19.64)	(1.69)	(.65)	(2.74)	(12.53)	(.18)	(.000)	(1.66)
WorkSec97	-.434	.126	-.100	-.111	-.453	-.027	-.223	-.155
	(19.81)	(.33)	(.30)	(.96)	(23.07)	(.02)	(1.33)	(2.24)
Nat r8185	.101	-.424	-.098	-.089	.111	-.310	-.088	-.057
	(1.13)	(.45)	(.33)	(.74)	(1.47)	(2.49)	(.26)	(.37)
Dist	-.571		-.487	-.772	-.712		-.552	-.802
	(40.10)		(8.08)	(88.65)	(66.80)		(15.59)	(114.40)
R^2	.835	.139	.398	.774	.846	.164	.384	.811
F	35.45	1.46	4.39	23.98	38.43	1.77	4.36	30.08
Non-Workers								
Soil	.074	.031	.266	.530	-.150	.242	.365	.454
	(.52)	(.02)	(2.66)	(9.26)	(3.40)	(1.37)	(11.33)	(6.56)
Lit7483	.870	-.032	.091	-.008	.657	.033	.314	-.008
	(33.29)	(.01)	(.18)	(.00)	(29.95)	(.01)	(1.95)	(.00)
WorkSec97	-.039	.185	.050	-.118	-.105	.053	-.195	-.158
	(.12)	(.71)	(.10)	(.40)	(1.41)	(.06)	(1.30)	(.70)
Nat r8185	.138	-.276	.200	-.230	-.270	-.270	.156	-.162
	(1.64)	(1.90)	(1.94)	(4.25)	(1.76)	(1.76)	(1.05)	(.89)
Dist	-.265		-.552	-.277	-.437		-.505	-.326
	(6.73)		(15.59)	(4.25)	(28.76)		(11.33)	(5.73)
R^2	.787	.128	.566	.396	.865	.097	.519	.424
F	25.93	1.32	(9.12)	4.59	44.96	.97	7.57	5.15

NOTE: $p < .05$ for underlined coefficients. F values in parentheses.

The difference between the results in the partial correlations and the regressions leads to less confidence in the accuracy of the proposed model than would otherwise occur. However, as the differing results in these two analyses illustrate, in multivariate analysis where the relation of each variable with *all* other variables in the analysis affects each coefficient, the interpretation of results is quite complicated.

The allocational migration rates to the two great cities and to Asiatic Russia can also be compared. Table 8.5 shows the correlations among the allocational rates and general out-migration. In the allocational rates, the number of migrants from a given origin to the given destination is divided by the number of out-migrants in thousands from the given origin, regardless of destination. The pattern of correlations is consistent with that in Table 8.1. Leaving the province of birth generally is seen as intermediate between choosing a modern urban destination and choosing an agricultural frontier destination. The correlations between the allocational migration rates to the two great cities and to Asiatic Russia shown in Table 8.5 are all negative, as was the case for the correlations between the simple migration rates to the two great cities and to Asiatic Russia shown in Table 8.1. However, in every case, the correlations in Table 8.5 are stronger than the corresponding correlations in Table 8.1. The stronger correlations between the allocational migration rates mean that provinces from which a large proportion of all migrants went to the two great cities sent a small proportion of migrants to Asiatic Russia. Such would not necessarily be the case. From Tables 2.6 and 2.7, it can be calculated that only 39 percent of migrants of each sex who were born in European Russia lived in Moscow City, St. Petersburg City, or Asiatic Russia in 1897. It would be possible that provinces could either send large

TABLE 8.5

CORRELATIONS AMONG ALLOCATIONAL MIGRATION RATES AND WITH GENERAL
OUT-MIGRATION RATE: 1897 (ON 41 PROVINCES)

	Male			Female		
	M-StP/Out	Outmig	AsRus/Out	M-StP/Out	Outmig	AsRus/Out
Total						
M-StP/Out	1.000	.427	-.544	1.000	.177	-.473
Outmig		1.000	-.030		1.000	.230
AsRus/Out			1.000			1.000
Workers						
M-StP/Out	1.000	.581	-.569	1.000	.681	-.479
Outmig		1.000	-.483		1.000	-.229
AsRus/Out			1.000			1.000
Non-Workers						
M-StP/Out	1.000	.210	-.461	1.000	-.088	-.464
Outmig		1.000	.273		1.000	.394
AsRus/Out			1.000			1.000

NOTE: $p <$ .05 for underlined coefficients, two-tailed tests.

proportions of migrants both to the two great cities and to
Asiatic Russia or alternatively that they could send only a
small proportion of migrants to either destination at the extremes of modernity and the bulk of migrants to minor destinations in European Russia close to the province of birth.

Tables 8.6 and 8.7 show the correlations and partial correlations between the allocational migration rates and the
non-distance explanatory variables used consistently in this
study. The general out-migration rate is also included in
Table 8.6. In neither table are there any exceptions to the
pattern of variation of coefficients of explanatory variables
according to the modernity of the destination, as sketched in
Figure 1.1. In each case, the greater the modernity of the
destination, the more negative the relation with soil fertility
and natural r and the more positive the relation with literacy

TABLE 8.6

CORRELATIONS OF ALLOCATIONAL MIGRATION RATES AND GENERAL OUT-MIGRATION
RATE WITH EXPLANATORY VARIABLES: 1897 (ON 41 PROVINCES)

	Male			Female		
	M-StP/Out	Outmig	AsRus/Out	M-StP/Out	Outmig	AsRus/Out
Total						
Soil	-.729*	.012	.451	-.751*	.187	.403
Lit7483	.807	.514	-.418*	.772	.261	-.361*
WorkSec97	.394	.415	-.288*	.385	.165	-.254*
Nat r8185	-.562*	-.481	.229*	-.562*	-.281	.175*
Workers						
Soil	-.738*	-.194	.295	-.727*	-.234	.328
Lit7483	.740*	.379	-.393*	.725*	.382	-.368*
WorkSec97	.301*	.071	-.231	.315*	.028	-.228
Nat r8185	-.544	-.497	.403*	-.542*	-.441	.273*
Non-Workers						
Soil	-.709*	.246	.441	-.752*	.374	.377
Lit7483	.865*	.332	-.365*	.800	.087	-.334*
WorkSec97	.518	.379	-.274*	.445	.101	-.248*
Nat r8185	-.567*	-.334	.137	-.572*	-.147	.143*

NOTE: p< .05 for underlined coefficients, two-tailed tests.

*Indicates that the magnitude of the coefficient in this table is greater than
the magnitude of the corresponding coefficient in Table 8.2.

and secondary industry. The results are generally similar to those in Tables 8.2 and 8.3. Those coefficients in Tables 8.6 and 8.7 whose magnitude is greater than the magnitude of the corresponding coefficients in Tables 8.2 or 8.3 are designated by an asterisk to the right of the coefficient.

For migration to Asiatic Russia, the allocational rates usually have a stronger relation with literacy and secondary industry than the simple rates, while for migration to the two great cities, the allocational rates usually have a stronger relation with soil fertility and natural r than the

TABLE 8.7

PARTIAL CORRELATIONS FOR ALLOCATIONAL MIGRATION RATES:
1897 (ON 41 PROVINCES)

	Male		Female	
	M-StP/Out	AsRus/Out	M-StP/Out	AsRus/Out
Total				
Soil	-.722*	.443	-.753*	.387
Lit7483	.699	-.500*	.636	-.439*
WorkSec97	.113	-.402*	.101	-.370*
Nat r8185	-.240*	.281*	-.243*	.219*
Workers				
Soil	-.728*	.244	-.747*	.319
Lit7483	.578*	-.469	.547*	-.556
WorkSec97	-.029	-.329	-.051	-.436
Nat r8185	-.216*	.499*	-.170*	.434*
Non-Workers				
Soil	-.670*	.420*	-.736*	.350*
Lit7483	.794*	-.412*	.684	-.397*
WorkSec97	.328	-.358*	.214	-.354*
Nat r8185	-.278*	.157	-.284*	.175

NOTE: $p < .05$ for underlined coefficients, two-tailed tests.
Coefficients are partialled on the appropriate distance measure.

*Indicates that the magnitude of the coefficient in this table is
greater than the magnitude of the corresponding coefficient in Table 8.3.

simple rates. These relations mean that provinces which
sent a large proportion of their migrants to Asiatic Russia
were generally lower in literacy and in the proportion of the
population working in secondary industry than were provinces which had high simple migration rates to Asiatic Russia. That is, it was significant if a province not only had a
high migration rate to Asiatic Russia but also if there were
relatively few migrants from that province who chose any
destination other than Asiatic Russia. On the other hand,

provinces which sent a large proportion of their migrant population to Moscow or St., Petersburg cities were lower in soil fertility and lower in natural r than were provinces which only had high simple migration rates to the two great cities.

These results of comparing allocational and simple migration rates suggest that, at least for migration to destinations at the extremes of modernity (the two great cities and Asiatic Russia), the migration decision process did not seem to be two-stage. It would have been a two-stage process if persons decided they wanted to migrate somewhere before they chose a particular destination or type of destination. If that were the case, out-migrants would be a more homogeneous group in terms of characteristics of origins than would be the total population that was born in European Russia according to the characteristics of province of birth.

If this two-stage process had been operating, then the relations of the allocational migration variables with each other in Table 8.5 and with the explanatory variables in Tables 8.6 and 8.7 would have been weaker than the corresponding relations with the simple migration variables in Tables 8.1 to 8.3. Instead, many relations are strengthened by comparing migrants to destinations of extreme degrees of modernity or lack of modernity with out-migrants as a group.

The allocational variables have strong relations with those explanatory variables that seem to be positive causes of migration to the destination at the opposite extreme of modernity, that is, the relation of M-StP with soil fertility and natural r in Tables 8.6 and 8.7 compared to the relation of M-StP with those explanatory variables in Tables 8.2 and 8.3. This pattern suggests that provinces which produced large numbers of migrants who chose the two great cities as destinations tended to produce a positive disinclination in their migrant population to move to Asiatic Russia. Similarly, those provinces which produced a large number of migrants to Asiatic Russia tended to have characteristics that were related to their migrant population being disinclined to move to the two great cities.

SUMMARY OF THE PERFORMANCE OF THE ORIGINAL HYPOTHESES

HYPOTHESES FOR MIGRATION WITHIN A SETTLED AREA

1. Migration rates are positively related to the cultural modernization of the place of origin.—Strong support.
2. Migration rates are positively related to the industrial modernization of the place of origin.—Partial support in correlations and partial correlations comparing migration rates to various destinations. Not supported generally for migration rates to particular destinations. Supported somewhat in the allocation of migrants between industrially modern and culturally modern destinations (Moscow versus St. Petersburg).
3. Migration rates are not strongly positively related to population pressure at the origin and thus are not mainly determined by such pressure.—Supported.
4. Migration rates are negatively related to the importance of traditional agriculture at the origin.—Supported.
5. Migration rates to specific destinations decrease with increasing difficulty of reaching the destination.—Supported.

HYPOTHESES FOR MIGRATION TO A FRONTIER AREA

6. Migration rates are negatively related to the cultural modernization of the origin.—Fairly strong support.
7. Migration rates are negatively related to the industrial modernization of the origin.—Partial support.
8. Migration rates are positively related to the importance of traditional agriculture at the origin.—Strong support.
9. Population pressure is strongly positively related to mi-

gration rates and is a main determinant of such rates.—
Strong support over time, supported in the correlations and
partial correlations comparing Asiatic Russia to other destinations. Not supported in lifetime migration to Asiatic
Russia considered alone.

10. If migration to a frontier area begins at a definite date,
then over time hypotheses 6-9 are increasingly more
strongly supported.—Supported or supported to some extent in all cases. Supported most strongly for natural r, less
strongly for soil fertility and literacy, and even less strongly
for secondary industry.

11. Migration rates decrease with increasing difficulty of
reaching the destination.—Supported for lifetime migration
to Asiatic Russia. Not supported for period migration to
Asiatic Russia.

HYPOTHESES CONCERNING RELATIVE DISTRIBUTION OF
MIGRANTS AMONG DESTINATIONS

12. The differences between characteristics of origins of
migrants to settled destinations and to frontier destinations
are also expected to appear in the relative distribution of
migrants between the two destinations.—Strong support.

CONCLUSIONS

The proposed model in this research worked fairly well
overall. However, this study has several limitations: it refers to only one society, and most of the data employed
were collected at the same point in time. Thus, it is not possible to determine whether migration patterns that seemed to
be related to the differential modernity of provinces of origin were in fact due to the differential progress of modernization in various provinces or whether the socio-economic
explanatory variables employed simply reflected long-

standing differences among areas that had little relation to the pace of socio-economic development in various regions. Many mechanisms assumed to be operating can only be verified by examining individual-level data, such as those in internal passports or collected at migration points. If this were done, the explicit contribution of ecological factors as compared to individual factors could be assessed.

The general applicability of the model can only be determined by additional tests of the model in other rapidly modernizing societies, such as late nineteenth- and early twentieth-century Japan. Japan also had an agricultural frontier, Hokkaido. It is expected that the model employed in a study of Japan would also differentiate sources of migration to Hokkaido from sources of migration to Tokyo and the other great Japanese cities. Currently developing countries such as Sri Lanka that have rural settlement programs would also provide appropriate test cases.

Although the model can be further tested, its implications for currently developing countries can also be considered. In this study, there are several such implications. If it is true that population pressure can motivate migration for agricultural settlement if the conditions of settlement are sufficiently clear, and if it is also true that this pressure does not generally motivate migration to major modern cities, then there are implications both for settlement programs and for programs to reduce overcrowding in cities, this major implication being that agricultural settlement programs can work to relieve crowding in rural areas where land is scarce but only if there are many assurances about the program that are understandable to the potential migrants. Also such a settlement program should not be expected to be immediately successful but should be allowed a period of at least five or ten years before it can be expected to attract substantial numbers of persons from the overcrowded rural areas.

Also such rural settlement programs should not be viewed as realistic alternatives to overcrowded cities if the types of persons and the types of areas of origins to which rural settlement programs appear attractive differ from the types of persons and areas to which an urban destination for migration appears attractive.

There are also implications for various types of rural industrialization programs. Rural industrialization has often been proposed as a method to promote more even geographic development in a country and as a way to employ potential migrants to cities within the rural area. Although rural industrialization may promote more even geographic development, it will not necessarily slow migration to cities. If the implications of this study are correct, the presence of rural industry may simply result in making many persons become migrants to urban places who never would have considered migrating to an urban area had not the rural industry been present. However, the findings for the Urals and Donbass areas suggest that extractive industry projects may serve as alternatives to rural settlement and thus may be another way to relieve overcrowding in rural areas. However, such extractive projects may be less likely to be viewed as an alternative to migration to major urban areas.

The findings about female migrants, although only suggestive, imply that women may not be as unimportant in the migration decision-making process as many researchers have assumed. Rather, women should be viewed as a labor source and should be assumed to behave much more like men in their responses to economic opportunities than has usually been the view of researchers.

Whether these implications for currently developing countries are valid is yet to be proved. However, further research may determine whether the model is correct historically and whether it has any applicability in today's world.

APPENDIX

This appendix contains various reference materials for the benefit of the interested reader. A map of European Russia with a key to provincial names is included. Also included are migration rates per thousand population from which the migration rates to the major destinations considered in this study can be computed. A listing of the values of the explanatory variables used consistently throughout this study along with a listing of the auxiliary occupation variable is also included.

The migration rate to European Russia is the migration rate out of the province of birth to anywhere else in European Russia. The migration rate to European Russia but not to Moscow or St. Petersburg cities and not to the Urals-Donbass can be computed by subtracting the migration rate to Moscow City, the migration rate to St. Petersburg City, and the migration rate to the Urals-Donbass from the migration rate to European Russia.

KEY TO MAP A.1 AND TABLE A.1

The following numbering system for provinces is used in Map A.1 and in Table A.1. The order is alphabetical in Russian. The numbers are the province identification numbers used in the vast majority of nineteenth-century Russian statistical publications.

1	Arkhangel	4	Vilna
2	Astrakhan	5	Vitebsk
3	Bessarabia	6	Vladimir

7	Vologda	29	Orel
8	Volhynia	30	Penza
9	Voronezh	31	Perm
10	Vyatka	32	Podolsk
11	Grodno	33	Poltava
12	Don	34	Pskov
13	Ekaterinoslav	35	Ryazan
14	Kazan	36	Samara
15	Kaluga	37	St. Petersburg
16	Kiev	38	Saratov
17	Kovno	39	Simbirsk
18	Kostroma	40	Smolensk
19	Kurland	41	Tavrida
20	Kursk	42	Tambov
21	Lifland	43	Tver
22	Minsk	44	Tula
23	Mogilev	45	Ufa
24	Moscow	46	Kharkov
25	Nizhni Novgorod	47	Kherson
26	Novgorod	48	Chernigov
27	Olonets	49	Estland
28	Orenburg	50	Yaroslavl

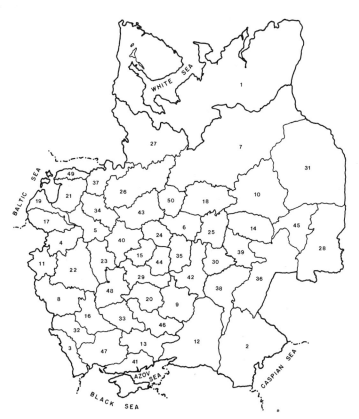

MAP A.1 Provinces of European Russia: 1897

TABLE A.1

VALUES OF EXPLANATORY VARIABLES AND MIGRATION RATES

Explanatory Variables

Province Number	Lit 7483	Soil	Agri w/aux	Nat r8185	WorkSec97
1	38	1	553.19	12	15
2	23	1	212.12	18	9
3	8	5	186.31	18	8
4	16	2	70.00	13	11
5	17	2	156.42	16	11
6	42	2	417.81	10	88
7	29	1	382.98	11	6
8	12	4	166.23	15	8
9	16	5	163.74	14	7
10	17	4	278.45	13	13
11	23	3	86.02	10	18
12	20	4	144.20	24	13
13	18	4	161.70	22	20
14	13	5	198.70	14	7
15	33	2	424.78	10	26
16	14	4	189.81	18	13
17	19	3	82.87	10	8
18	37	2	472.39	10	45
19	60	2	94.74	10	23
20	17	5	207.61	8	10
21	95	2	130.95	9	41
22	19	3	168.00	17	9
23	14	3	204.76	21	8
24	53	2	359.65	4	156
25	23	3	415.30	9	24
26	33	1	401.10	9	12
27	28	1	509.43	10	10
28	13	4	169.72	18	7
29	21	4	195.83	11	19
30	12	5	207.07	14	10
31	17	3	302.87	12	20
32	11	5	188.86	17	6
33	13	5	185.60	17	6
34	20	1	136.99	12	4
35	30	4	224.49	13	28
36	14	4	98.73	18	6
37	59	1	295.92	-1	97
38	19	5	172.19	13	12
39	18	5	222.22	12	11
40	24	2	262.03	13	11
41	24	4	117.95	20	16
42	16	5	192.77	15	10
43	41	1	353.77	12	25
44	33	4	213.41	11	18
45	7	4	149.25	19	5
46	14	5	139.82	16	13
47	24	4	125.00	15	20
48	19	4	197.28	15	12
49	95	2	166.67	7	37
50	63	2	336.28	7	42

General Outmigration Rate

Province Number	M	F	MW	FW	MNW	FNW
1	100.32	76.32	358.08	374.27	69.79	58.56
2	76.02	62.08	171.94	188.57	63.82	58.94
3	50.92	34.92	102.53	97.98	47.81	33.32
4	102.85	68.88	253.43	143.53	86.22	63.95
5	112.84	77.76	386.54	240.39	85.79	68.39
6	154.92	86.20	291.49	212.42	119.66	74.32
7	75.15	44.74	481.92	319.52	52.05	35.94
8	60.86	37.25	167.75	125.32	54.16	34.39
9	162.54	130.33	464.12	385.51	138.92	123.67
10	112.19	68.00	369.62	255.82	91.20	63.99
11	93.23	56.62	224.26	131.30	80.15	52.85
12	73.13	48.14	290.12	127.99	59.09	45.87
13	100.30	86.08	274.27	190.60	86.46	82.22
14	97.55	63.06	488.58	243.55	72.51	59.47
15	244.46	120.43	620.85	533.87	156.76	96.14
16	88.52	64.21	244.07	164.50	75.00	59.67
17	121.34	81.33	229.22	140.08	99.93	73.36
18	124.97	55.70	316.69	186.43	94.92	46.73
19	204.61	175.23	216.91	190.89	199.59	172.33
20	173.00	126.79	488.53	409.64	138.65	117.10
21	126.67	100.79	103.59	72.16	134.66	106.99
22	77.12	48.75	208.61	140.63	67.13	44.74
23	100.63	61.48	356.07	261.34	82.30	54.64
24	105.41	80.90	104.27	93.52	105.80	79.28
25	107.99	56.64	305.12	164.51	80.28	52.94
26	95.41	87.36	499.19	460.98	53.39	60.91
27	90.05	63.35	399.97	426.30	61.64	46.91
28	69.42	49.04	130.32	157.48	64.57	46.89
29	162.15	105.32	494.76	399.87	112.36	94.56
30	158.82	107.03	494.78	358.91	123.81	100.15
31	75.98	49.68	117.96	95.34	70.35	47.90
32	77.51	51.24	248.65	170.01	65.02	46.85
33	157.68	125.43	395.25	244.37	133.86	118.99
34	97.50	65.16	572.82	442.86	57.74	48.22
35	206.19	124.95	559.15	473.25	136.47	103.23
36	97.36	74.86	248.55	220.26	87.55	71.47
37	100.49	89.61	123.79	110.10	96.65	87.64
38	103.99	73.51	259.94	238.58	89.74	67.72
39	126.76	81.19	412.10	280.53	98.92	75.13
40	142.28	79.94	567.58	424.72	79.81	61.67
41	95.93	89.90	182.67	145.34	90.03	87.91
42	133.13	90.65	398.20	315.71	107.88	85.21
43	181.16	110.83	556.63	454.35	107.23	82.64
44	192.73	130.17	551.64	615.82	121.05	101.01
45	61.72	39.77	249.31	212.27	50.41	37.51
46	132.00	101.54	387.18	272.28	109.14	94.86
47	63.35	57.56	124.23	102.84	58.36	55.55
48	139.09	97.61	378.40	218.50	114.62	91.80
49	119.44	109.69	122.81	125.21	118.43	107.41
50	225.93	95.64	528.35	307.28	153.17	79.24

Lifetime Migration Rate to Moscow

Province Number	M	F	MW	FW	MNW	FNW
1	1.96	1.52	5.74	7.83	1.51	1.14
2	0.55	0.50	1.40	8.25	0.44	0.31
3	0.44	0.19	2.27	3.37	0.33	0.11
4	2.21	0.88	6.77	4.16	1.71	0.66
5	1.58	1.06	9.16	6.08	0.83	0.77
6	42.57	27.67	82.95	83.62	32.15	22.40
7	2.77	2.39	18.11	30.25	1.90	1.50
8	0.88	0.24	5.86	2.73	0.57	0.16
9	1.58	0.98	14.34	13.75	0.58	0.64
10	1.60	0.33	13.23	4.76	0.65	0.24
11	2.90	0.79	20.31	5.79	1.16	0.54
12	1.51	0.70	11.85	8.13	0.84	0.49
13	0.52	0.45	2.53	3.92	0.36	0.32
14	1.66	0.82	10.28	14.56	1.10	0.54
15	70.76	32.74	211.12	304.99	38.06	16.75
16	0.84	0.56	3.69	5.01	0.59	0.36
17	1.52	0.79	6.31	2.29	0.57	0.59
18	6.24	4.02	38.63	28.50	1.16	2.34
19	3.61	3.04	5.93	7.53	2.66	2.21
20	1.24	1.16	5.91	12.12	0.74	0.79
21	2.87	2.99	3.55	6.16	2.64	2.30
22	1.37	0.73	11.95	5.39	0.56	0.52
23	1.85	1.51	14.05	17.02	0.97	0.98
24	--	--	--	--	--	--
25	4.64	1.49	19.28	20.13	2.58	0.85
26	1.53	1.52	9.98	8.66	0.65	1.01
27	1.97	0.50	12.11	4.53	1.04	0.32
28	0.65	0.31	4.66	6.10	0.33	0.20
29	4.01	1.85	18.79	22.79	1.80	1.08
30	1.86	1.50	14.19	19.73	0.57	1.00
31	0.74	0.25	2.60	1.93	0.49	0.18
32	0.69	0.19	3.18	2.13	0.51	0.11
33	1.00	0.39	5.04	2.59	0.59	0.27
34	0.93	0.73	7.61	6.18	0.38	0.48
35	42.73	22.43	199.37	215.42	11.79	10.42
36	0.50	0.33	5.57	4.48	0.17	0.23
37	7.50	7.85	31.43	34.20	3.56	5.31
38	1.03	0.91	4.11	9.29	0.75	0.62
39	2.81	1.10	17.79	15.57	1.35	0.66
40	35.71	14.74	197.78	195.88	11.90	5.14
41	1.65	0.76	8.45	6.56	1.19	0.55
42	3.23	2.41	22.30	44.11	1.42	1.40
43	20.18	9.75	108.08	97.61	2.87	2.54
44	54.07	33.57	249.16	355.55	15.10	14.23
45	0.63	0.18	6.41	5.33	0.28	0.11
46	1.41	0.80	12.04	8.47	0.46	0.50
47	0.86	0.91	5.37	6.07	0.49	0.68
48	1.18	1.27	7.25	6.21	0.56	1.03
49	1.97	2.42	4.47	6.35	1.22	1.85
50	30.63	11.97	64.65	72.84	22.44	7.25

NOTE: -- Not applicable

Lifetime Migration Rate to St. Petersburg

Province Number	M	F	MW	FW	MNW	FNW
1	32.01	25.38	178.63	198.84	14.64	15.04
2	2.76	0.73	1.16	1.77	2.96	0.70
3	0.67	0.34	0.51	0.92	0.68	0.33
4	10.89	5.51	54.70	22.76	6.05	4.37
5	25.20	15.42	171.10	111.26	10.78	9.89
6	4.73	2.79	10.60	6.90	3.25	2.41
7	12.96	7.35	139.85	1C2.04	5.76	4.32
8	0.75	0.38	1.89	1.69	0.68	0.33
9	1.99	0.68	3.83	3.40	1.85	0.61
10	1.06	0.33	3.04	3.30	0.90	0.27
11	2.79	1.60	8.89	5.40	2.19	1.41
12	2.50	0.54	1.56	1.28	2.56	0.52
13	1.55	0.58	1.99	1.64	1.51	0.54
14	1.54	0.82	19.33	6.35	0.40	0.71
15	19.42	8.91	51.85	47.48	11.86	6.64
16	1.68	0.75	2.53	1.29	1.61	0.72
17	8.53	4.90	35.35	11.26	3.21	4.04
18	28.09	11.01	84.96	42.86	19.18	8.83
19	10.07	8.56	7.68	9.54	11.05	8.38
20	1.10	0.85	2.94	4.98	0.90	0.71
21	13.29	12.78	14.54	15.31	12.86	12.23
22	3.05	1.22	12.00	5.61	2.37	1.03
23	2.73	1.81	11.60	8.34	2.09	1.59
24	15.42	12.72	22.77	24.58	12.90	11.21
25	5.90	2.47	20.08	11.69	3.91	2.15
26	44.97	51.52	368.69	366.24	11.28	29.24
27	41.05	32.06	262.30	340.65	20.76	18.09
28	0.80	0.40	1.10	2.30	0.78	0.37
29	2.04	1.69	6.52	12.15	1.37	1.31
30	2.55	1.35	10.65	10.56	1.71	1.10
31	1.10	0.39	1.02	1.20	1.11	0.36
32	1.17	0.41	2.32	1.17	1.09	0.38
33	1.01	0.68	2.02	1.69	0.91	0.62
34	47.57	33.59	438.17	355.06	14.90	19.17
35	21.39	9.16	92.73	46.53	7.30	6.84
36	2.09	0.54	3.12	5.49	2.02	0.42
37	--	--	--	--	--	--
38	2.30	0.88	3.51	4.10	2.19	0.77
39	3.18	0.94	7.63	5.16	2.75	0.81
40	23.41	13.37	125.93	110.10	8.36	8.24
41	1.40	1.09	2.90	1.53	1.30	1.08
42	3.11	1.46	12.48	12.69	2.21	1.19
43	86.23	52.05	328.34	276.56	38.55	33.62
44	10.39	6.66	38.15	38.09	4.85	4.77
45	0.56	0.22	1.09	2.85	0.53	0.19
46	0.97	0.77	1.79	2.08	0.90	0.72
47	1.46	1.15	1.08	1.40	1.49	1.14
48	1.15	0.75	1.96	2.40	1.06	0.67
49	22.34	29.66	29.32	60.29	20.24	25.17
50	127.67	43.25	378.57	172.56	67.30	33.23

NOTE: -- Not applicable

Lifetime Migration Rate to Asiatic Russia

Province Number	M	F	MW	FW	MNW	FNW
1	9.44	6.38	21.69	7.46	7.99	6.31
2	24.40	21.56	62.54	39.49	19.54	21.11
3	2.86	1.11	15.08	1.84	2.13	1.09
4	5.52	2.59	14.46	3.15	4.53	2.55
5	9.42	6.48	21.89	7.16	8.19	6.44
6	11.75	5.34	17.83	5.13	10.18	5.36
7	8.74	6.12	29.68	14.05	7.55	5.87
8	4.60	1.49	19.31	2.75	3.68	1.45
9	34.86	28.97	40.47	24.94	34.42	29.07
10	27.21	19.23	83.11	54.20	22.65	18.48
11	6.60	3.28	15.54	3.01	5.71	3.29
12	8.14	5.78	24.16	10.56	7.11	5.64
13	6.25	3.84	16.58	6.40	5.43	3.75
14	18.45	12.76	85.87	40.67	14.13	12.21
15	11.12	5.00	17.58	5.13	9.61	4.99
16	6.60	3.09	20.46	4.89	5.39	3.01
17	8.39	2.56	11.43	1.84	7.78	2.65
18	7.01	3.30	14.99	4.14	5.77	3.25
19	5.80	2.81	5.03	1.02	6.11	3.14
20	37.93	32.27	32.30	21.45	38.55	32.64
21	6.19	2.50	8.00	1.02	5.57	2.83
22	3.98	1.58	13.38	2.71	3.27	1.53
23	4.38	2.31	15.38	3.88	3.59	2.25
24	7.24	2.94	9.40	2.09	6.51	3.04
25	18.79	10.29	62.17	25.43	12.69	9.77
26	4.52	1.95	13.14	2.29	3.62	1.93
27	5.31	3.92	9.77	5.45	4.90	3.85
28	35.55	28.64	74.81	80.93	32.42	27.61
29	21.73	16.99	24.65	18.67	21.30	16.93
30	37.38	30.92	61.20	39.29	34.90	30.69
31	43.48	30.58	76.27	56.57	39.08	29.57
32	6.59	2.12	22.78	4.46	5.41	2.03
33	36.70	30.73	28.22	16.99	37.55	31.47
34	6.84	4.48	15.65	3.09	6.10	4.54
35	24.98	19.82	22.68	10.50	25.44	20.39
36	31.70	26.62	87.50	58.32	28.08	25.88
37	9.06	3.81	15.79	2.29	7.95	3.95
38	21.57	13.48	47.81	29.09	19.17	12.93
39	20.85	13.03	80.60	32.46	15.02	12.44
40	12.01	6.19	22.57	6.16	10.46	6.19
41	6.23	4.20	22.94	6.88	5.10	4.10
42	34.43	29.09	49.42	36.74	33.00	28.91
43	4.36	1.67	9.54	2.52	3.34	1.60
44	13.84	9.03	17.25	8.81	13.16	9.05
45	10.47	7.43	48.32	33.44	8.19	7.09
46	16.38	11.05	21.56	11.10	15.91	11.05
47	6.89	3.64	20.00	5.41	5.81	3.56
48	35.18	29.51	29.80	12.10	35.74	30.35
49	5.96	2.00	10.01	1.14	4.74	2.12
50	6.41	2.19	10.31	2.86	5.47	2.14

Period Migration Rates to Asiatic Russia

Province Number	1885-89	1890-94	1895-99	1900-04	1905-09
1	0.0	0.0	0.10	0.50	0.0
2	0.0	0.01	0.50	0.13	0.83
3	0.0	0.0	0.80	1.31	11.29
4	0.01	0.08	5.64	6.97	7.22
5	1.05	0.06	15.33	19.10	38.78
6	0.0	0.01	0.15	0.06	0.26
7	0.0	0.01	1.31	1.95	5.84
8	0.0	0.0	1.24	1.74	8.29
9	0.56	11.59	11.59	6.32	36.80
10	2.92	7.33	5.09	2.96	8.97
11	0.04	0.29	4.52	3.19	3.98
12	0.0	0.01	1.56	1.52	8.40
13	0.0	0.02	3.67	9.31	30.25
14	1.22	3.50	2.33	0.67	4.09
15	0.0	0.01	3.57	0.59	12.83
16	0.0	0.01	2.90	3.91	29.15
17	0.0	0.0	0.54	0.25	1.17
18	0.0	0.02	0.42	0.63	3.94
19	0.0	0.01	2.57	0.54	1.67
20	15.81	16.93	20.44	9.58	44.69
21	0.0	0.0	3.59	2.09	3.60
22	0.12	0.21	4.52	5.78	19.61
23	0.24	0.10	10.77	19.99	58.08
24	0.0	0.0	0.04	0.01	0.06
25	0.65	3.46	1.37	0.63	2.04
26	0.0	0.0	0.65	0.08	1.03
27	0.0	0.0	0.0	0.03	0.0
28	0.0	0.01	1.13	0.46	5.91
29	1.46	3.77	21.34	4.05	30.23
30	0.75	5.57	25.68	4.83	15.80
31	3.21	5.88	3.40	2.31	3.34
32	0.0	0.0	0.26	2.43	11.12
33	1.19	16.81	28.58	19.57	45.95
34	0.0	0.0	2.17	3.74	9.64
35	0.25	7.90	8.52	1.10	8.82
36	0.77	1.83	15.53	2.78	19.86
37	0.0	0.0	0.09	0.06	0.95
38	0.17	4.74	6.89	2.48	14.40
39	0.13	3.70	7.24	1.79	5.52
40	0.34	0.01	5.17	3.61	17.34
41	0.0	0.05	2.21	9.05	32.39
42	2.82	14.55	15.59	3.89	19.71
43	0.0	0.0	0.28	0.20	1.03
44	0.03	1.21	12.36	1.32	6.38
45	0.0	0.01	2.33	1.03	5.21
46	2.12	3.54	9.76	9.27	30.50
47	0.0	0.00	4.22	6.22	15.45
48	0.46	7.24	31.69	12.64	49.07
49	0.0	0.0	0.09	0.73	6.46
50	0.0	0.0	0.01	0.0	0.0

Lifetime Migration Rate within European Russia

Province Number	M	F	MW	FW	MNW	FNW
1	87.35	64.17	333.99	363.95	58.14	46.30
2	37.61	26.75	76.99	85.99	32.61	25.28
3	31.83	29.65	77.31	89.57	29.09	28.13
4	87.60	61.45	223.93	130.52	72.55	56.88
5	98.06	68.84	357.04	228.47	72.46	59.64
6	126.61	77.10	264.65	204.10	90.97	65.14
7	61.56	38.05	447.82	302.38	39.63	29.59
8	43.50	32.13	132.22	111.34	37.94	29.55
9	67.33	57.25	249.73	202.92	53.04	53.45
10	81.55	47.86	279.36	195.54	65.42	44.70
11	58.61	35.41	149.40	83.13	49.54	33.00
12	33.26	21.77	68.29	61.81	30.99	20.63
13	57.32	49.69	189.37	131.11	46.82	46.68
14	71.01	48.02	379.59	185.70	51.25	45.28
15	208.98	109.03	584.64	518.76	121.46	84.95
16	68.98	54.82	204.70	149.85	57.19	50.52
17	94.26	72.93	207.37	132.95	71.81	64.79
18	114.02	51.69	298.85	181.18	85.05	42.81
19	185.87	169.41	209.40	188.30	176.25	165.91
20	95.46	65.97	355.70	309.10	67.14	57.64
21	107.73	95.48	92.32	69.95	113.06	101.01
22	64.89	43.16	181.10	126.30	56.06	39.53
23	87.92	55.40	324.78	248.88	70.92	48.78
24	81.88	74.85	91.93	89.57	78.42	72.97
25	77.67	42.99	218.70	126.57	57.85	40.12
26	88.93	84.45	482.96	456.82	47.92	58.09
27	82.95	58.58	386.92	418.52	55.08	42.27
28	27.90	18.82	49.01	67.73	26.21	17.85
29	117.68	73.65	420.03	328.10	72.43	64.36
30	99.39	68.51	375.71	278.24	70.59	62.77
31	29.04	18.62	40.22	37.10	27.54	17.90
32	66.13	46.84	216.12	161.93	55.18	42.59
33	74.52	56.77	281.19	185.97	53.80	49.77
34	87.11	59.70	553.49	437.12	48.10	42.77
35	156.21	97.61	511.34	449.14	86.06	75.73
36	56.10	42.38	126.52	130.71	51.53	40.32
37	83.45	79.94	103.68	103.64	80.11	77.66
38	61.15	47.94	156.41	160.46	52.45	43.99
39	95.86	63.95	297.39	226.09	76.20	59.02
40	121.96	71.60	537.54	413.95	60.91	53.46
41	67.89	65.55	116.44	109.02	64.59	63.99
42	71.96	53.01	287.22	235.35	51.46	48.61
43	172.59	108.23	544.00	450.20	99.46	80.16
44	161.32	115.05	517.74	595.21	90.14	86.21
45	47.34	31.84	196.12	173.93	38.37	29.98
46	61.25	50.37	239.99	169.72	45.24	45.70
47	43.26	45.98	88.79	87.92	39.53	44.12
48	71.72	48.90	290.32	177.09	49.36	42.74
49	97.51	102.83	109.17	120.47	93.99	100.25
50	215.92	91.63	514.63	301.36	144.05	75.37

Lifetime Migration Rate to Urals-Donbass Provinces

Province Number	M	F	MW	FW	MNW	FNW
1	2.48	2.05	6.99	4.88	1.95	1.88
2	6.55	6.43	21.28	21.12	4.68	6.06
3	1.22	1.16	1.85	1.49	1.18	1.15
4	3.00	2.04	8.19	2.85	2.42	1.99
5	3.50	2.61	8.88	3.83	2.97	2.54
6	10.34	5.90	12.17	3.85	9.87	6.09
7	7.72	3.85	80.58	26.82	3.58	3.12
8	1.18	.85	4.94	2.48	.94	.79
9	39.36	32.43	170.43	120.51	29.10	30.13
10	30.93	17.32	180.31	85.11	18.75	15.87
11	3.06	1.79	10.29	4.11	2.33	1.67
12	6.02	5.67	20.97	21.85	5.05	5.21
13	16.74	16.57	41.34	33.54	14.79	15.94
14	17.23	10.13	119.85	29.97	10.66	9.73
15	17.34	8.91	49.08	14.49	10.56	8.58
16	6.31	4.93	22.64	11.32	4.89	4.64
17	3.26	2.03	4.84	1.47	2.95	2.11
18	6.00	2.82	9.76	2.83	5.41	2.82
19	3.16	2.02	2.68	.48	3.36	2.31
20	30.07	19.53	136.76	73.42	18.46	17.69
21	1.96	1.13	1.46	.64	2.13	1.24
22	5.52	3.96	21.47	11.38	4.31	3.63
23	11.88	5.86	92.57	20.59	6.09	5.35
24	4.30	3.15	4.33	1.80	4.29	3.32
25	10.05	6.06	39.34	13.71	5.94	5.80
26	.93	.75	2.92	1.14	.72	.72
27	1.01	.84	3.21	1.16	.80	.83
28	6.02	5.53	16.68	20.02	5.17	5.24
29	34.99	19.64	161.24	86.28	16.09	17.20
30	14.48	10.76	44.66	26.98	11.34	10.32
31	8.26	7.91	22.96	14.72	6.29	7.64
32	1.42	.81	2.12	4.83	1.37	.66
33	22.82	20.95	78.37	50.09	17.52	19.37
34	1.05	.86	1.90	1.68	.98	.82
35	18.31	12.32	45.50	19.25	12.94	11.88
36	18.57	17.23	45.19	32.55	16.85	16.87
37	3.87	3.70	3.82	2.15	3.87	3.85
38	13.15	11.04	31.08	22.37	11.51	10.64
39	11.75	8.71	32.34	17.81	9.74	8.43
40	11.51	4.16	65.25	8.94	3.61	3.91
41	33.16	34.72	52.74	48.87	31.83	34.21
42	19.58	13.28	86.76	42.63	13.19	12.58
43	1.48	1.08	2.92	1.33	1.20	1.06
44	20.28	12.05	65.01	22.19	11.34	11.44
45	22.57	19.36	139.38	99.45	15.53	18.31
46	33.77	27.81	169.43	102.30	21.62	24.90
47	7.16	7.52	16.44	10.80	6.40	7.37
48	13.94	7.82	66.35	19.03	8.58	7.28
49	.73	.76	.80	.75	.71	.76
50	1.65	1.00	2.19	1.12	1.52	.99

NOTE: Rates for provinces 12, 13, 28 and 31 are migration rates to the other three Urals-Donbass provinces.

BIBLIOGRAPHY

Abu-Lughod, J. 1971. *Cairo: 1001 Years of the City Victorious*. Princeton: Princeton University Press.

Anderson, B. 1974. *Internal Migration in a Modernizing Society: The Case of Late Nineteenth Century European Russia*. Ph.D. dissertation, Princeton University.

————. 1977. Who Chose the Cities?: Migrants to Moscow and St. Petersburg in the Late Nineteenth Century. In *Population Patterns in the Past*, ed. R. Lee. New York: Academic Press.

Anderson, B., and McCabe J. 1977. Nutrition and the Fertility of Younger Women in Kinshasa, Zaïre. *Journal of Development Economics* 4(4):343-363.

Bendix, R. 1967. Preconditions of Development: A Comparison of Japan and Germany. In *Aspects of Social Change in Modern Japan*, ed. R. L. Dore. Princeton: Princeton University Press.

Black, C. 1966. *The Dynamics of Modernization*. New York: Harper & Row.

————, et al. 1975. *The Modernization of Japan and Russia*. New York: The Free Press

Blackwell, W. L. 1968. *The Beginnings of Russian Industrialization, 1800-1860*. Princeton: Princeton University Press.

————. 1970. *The Industrialization of Russia: An Historical Perspective*. New York: Thomas Y. Crowell Company.

Blum, J. 1961. *Lord and Peasant in Russia from the Ninth to the Nineteenth Century*. Princeton: Princeton University Press.

Boserup, E. 1970. *The Conditions of Agricultural Growth*. New York: St. Martin's Press.

Browning, H., and Feindt, W. 1969. Selectivity of Migrants to a Metropolis in a Developing Country. *Demography* 6(4):347-357.

Burch, T. 1962. *Internal Migration in Venezuela: A Methodological Study*. Ph.D. dissertation, Princeton University.

Byerlee, D. 1972. Research on Migration in Africa: Past, Present, and Future. East Lansing African Rural Employment Paper No. 2, Department of Agricultural Economics, Michigan State University.

Chamratrithirung, A. 1976. *Fertility, Nuptiality, and Migration in Thailand, 1970 Census: The Multiphasic Response Theory*. Ph.D. dissertation, Brown University.

Chi, P., and Bogan, M. 1974. A Study of Migrants and Return-Migrants in Peru. Paper presented at the annual meeting of the Population Association of America in New York, April.

Coale, A. 1973. The Demographic Transition Reconsidered. In *International Population Conference, Liège, 1973*. Liège, Belgium: International Union for the Scientific Study of Population.

Coale, A., Anderson, B., and Härm, E. 1979. *Human Fertility in Russia Since the Nineteenth Century*. Princeton: Princeton University Press.

Crisp, O. 1976. *Studies in the Russian Economy Before 1914*. London: Macmillan.

Davis, K. 1963. The Theory of Change and Response in Modern Demographic History. *Population Index* 29(4):345-366.

Davtyan, L. 1966. The Influence of Socio-Economic Factors on Natality. In *Proceedings of the World Population Conference 1965*. New York: World Population Conference, Belgrade, pp. 73-77.

Demko, G. 1969. *The Russian Colonization of Kazakhstan, 1896-1916*. Bloomington: Indiana University Press.

Dubnow, S. M. 1975. *History of the Jews in Russia and Poland from the Earliest Times until the Present Day*. 3 vols. New York: KTAV Publishing House reprint of publication of the Jewish Publication Society of America, 1916-1920.

Duncan, O. 1975. *Introduction to Structural Equation Models*. New York: Academic Press.

Eisenstadt, S. N. 1966. *Modernization: Protest and Change*. Englewood Cliffs: Prentice-Hall.

Fedor, T. 1975. *Patterns of Urban Growth in the Russian Empire During the Nineteenth Century*. Chicago: Research Paper No. 163, Department of Geography, University of Chicago.

Fields, G. 1975. Rural-Urban Migration, Urban Unemployment, and Job Search Activity in the LDC's, *Journal of Development Economics* 2(2):165-187.

Flinn, W. L., and Converse, J. W. 1970. Eight Assumptions Concerning Rural-Urban Migration in Colombia: A Three-Shantytowns Test. *Land Economics* 46(4):456-466.

Florinsky, M. T. 1953. *Russia*. 2 vols. New York: The Macmillan Company.

Friedlander, D. 1969. Demographic Responses and Population Change. *Demography* 6(4):359-381.

Geertz, C. 1963. *Agricultural Involution: The Process of Ecological Change in Indonesia*. Berkeley: University of California Press.

Gilbert, M. 1972. *Russian History Atlas*. New York: The Macmillan Company.

Goldstein, S. 1971. Interrelation Between Migration and Fertility in Population Redistribution in Thailand. Bangkok: Research Report No. 5, Institute of Population Studies, Chulalonghorn University.

————. 1973a. The Effect of Broken Marriage on Fertility Levels in Thailand. Paper presented at the annual meeting of the Population Association of America in New Orleans, April 27-30.

————. 1973b. Interrelations Between Migration and Fertility in Thailand. *Demography* 10(2):225-241.

Granovetter, M. 1974. *Getting a Job*. Cambridge: Harvard University Press.

Greenwood, M. J. 1969. The Determinants of Labor Migration in Egypt. *Journal of Regional Science* 9(2):283-290.

Grossman, G. 1973. Russia and the Soviet Union. In *The Fontana Economic History of Europe: The Emergence of Industrial Societies*, vol. 4, pt. 2, ed. C. M. Cipolla. London: Collins/Fontana Books.

Gugler, J. 1969. On the Theory of Rural-Urban Migration: The Case of Sub-Saharan Africa. In *Migration*, ed. J. A. Jackson. London: Cambridge University Press.

Harris, J., and Todaro, M. 1970. Migration, Unemployment, and Development: A Two-Sector Analysis. *American Economic Review* 60(1):126-142.

Hendershot, G. E. 1971. Cityward Migration and Urban Fertility in the Philippines. *Philippine Sociological Review* 5(6):845-927.

Herrick, B. H. 1965. *Urban Migration and Economic Development in Chile*. Cambridge: Massachusetts Institute of Technology Press.

Iamzin, I. 1912. *Pereselencheskoe Dvizhenie s Momenta Osvobozhdeniia Krestian* [Migratory movement from the time of the emancipation of the serfs]. Kiev: Tip. I Universiteta.

Ignatovich, I. 1900. Pomeshchich'i krest'iane nakanune osvobozhdeniia [Estate peasants on the eve of the emancipation]. *Russkoe Bogatsvo* 9-10.

Inkeles, A., and Smith, D. 1974. *Becoming Modern*. Cambridge: Harvard University Press.

Isard, W. 1960. *Methods of Regional Analysis: An Introduction to Regional Science*. New York: The Technology Press of the Massachusetts Institute of Technology and John Wiley & Sons.

Johnson, R. 1976. Peasant Migration and the Russian Working Class: Moscow at the End of the Nineteenth Century. *Slavic Review* 35(4):652-664.

Jorgenson, D. W. 1961. The Development of the Dual Economy. *Economic Journal* 71:309-334.

Kabuzan, V. M. 1971. *Izmeneniia v Razmeshchenii Naseleniia Rossii* [Changes in the distribution of the population of Russia]. Moscow: Nauka.

Kemper, R. V. 1971. Rural-Urban Migration in Latin America: A Framework for the Comparative Analysis of Geographical and Temporal Patterns. *International Migration Review* 5(2):36-47.

Kuznets, S. 1964. Introduction: Population Redistribution, Migration, and Economic Growth. In *Population Redistribution and Economic Growth: United States 1850-1950*, vol. 3. Philadelphia: The American Philosophical Society.

————. 1966. *Modern Economic Growth: Rate, Structure, and Spread*. New Haven: Yale University Press.

Leasure, J. W., and Lewis, R. A. 1968. Internal Migration in Russia in the Late Nineteenth Century. *Slavic Review* 27(3):375-394.

Lesthaeghe, R. 1971. Nuptiality and Population Growth. *Population Studies* 25(3):415-432.

Levy, M. J., Jr. 1966. *Modernization and the Structure of Societies*. Princeton: Princeton University Press.

———. 1972. *Modernization: Latecomers and Survivors*. New York: Basic Books.

Levy, M., and Wadycki, W. 1973. The Influence of Friends and Relatives on Geographic Labor Migration: An International Comparison. *Review of Economics and Statistics* 55(2):198-203.

Lewis, W. A. 1954. Economic Development with Unlimited Supplies of Labor. *The Manchester School* 22(2):139-191.

———. 1955. *The Theory of Economic Growth*. Homewood: Richard D. Irwin, Inc.

Long, L. H. 1973. Migration Differentials by Education and Occupation: Trends and Variations. *Demography* 10(2):243-258.

Lydolph, P. E. 1970. *The Geography of the U.S.S.R*. New York: John Wiley & Sons.

Marczewski, J. 1963. The Take-off Hypothesis and French Experience. In *The Economics of Take-off Into Sustained Growth*, ed. W. W. Rostow. New York: St. Martin's Press.

Mavor, J. 1914. *An Economic History of Russia*. 2 vols. London: J. M. Dent and Sons.

McBride, T. 1976. *The Domestic Revolution: The Modernization of Household Service in England and France*. New York: Holmes and Meier.

McCutcheon, L. 1977. *Migrant Adjustment in Surabaya, Indonesia*. Ph.D. dissertation, Brown University.

McKeown, T. 1976. *The Modern Rise of Population*. New York: Academic Press.

Mendoza-Pascual, E. 1966. *Population Redistribution in the Philippines*. Manila: University of the Philippines Population Institute.

Moscow (City) Statisticheskii Otdel. 1885-1886. *Perepis Moskvi 1882 Goda* [Moscow (City) census of 1882]. Moscow: Moscow Gorodshaiia Tipografia.

Mosher, W. 1978. *The Theory of Change and Response: A Case Study of Puerto Rico, with Application to Sweden*. Ph.D. dissertation, Brown University.

Notestein, F. 1945. Population—The Long View. In *Food for the World*, ed. T. Schultz. Chicago: University of Chicago Press.

Parker, W. H. 1969. *An Historical Geography of Russia*. Chicago: Aldine Publishing Company.

Parsons, T. 1953. A Revised Analytical Approach to the Theory of Social Stratification. In *Class, Status and Power*, ed. R. Bendix and S. M. Lipset. Glencoe: The Free Press.

———. 1964. A Functional Theory of Social Change. In *Social Change,* ed. A. Etzioni and E. Etzioni. New York: Basic Books.

Petersen, W. 1958. A General Typology of Migration. *American Sociological Review* 23(3):256-266.

Pipes, R. 1974. *Russia Under the Old Regime*. New York: Charles Scribner's Sons.

Polotov, S. T. 1963. *Rabochie Donbassa v XIX Veke* [Workers of the Donbass in the nineteenth century]. Moscow: Izdatelstvo Akademia Nauk.

Population Studies and Training Center, Brown University. 1978. Comparative Studies of Migrant Adjustment in Asian Cities. *International Migration Review* 12(1). Articles by S. Goldstein, S. Green, G. Hendershot, L. McCutcheon, A. Speare, and P. Tirasawat.

Rashin, A. G. 1940. *Formirovanie Promishlennogo Pro-letariata v Rossii* [Formation of the Industrial Proletariat in Russia]. Moscow: Sotzetliz.

———. 1956. *Naselenie Rossii za 100 Let* [The population of Russia for 100 years]. Moscow: Gosstatizdat.

Redfield, R., and Rojas, A. 1962. *Chan Kom: A Maya Village*. Chicago: University of Chicago Press.

Robinson, G. T. 1969. *Rural Russia Under the Old Regime*. 2nd ed. Berkeley: University of California Press.

Rozman, G. 1976. *Urban Networks in Russia and Premodern Periodization, 1750-1800*. Princeton: Princeton University Press.

Russia, Tzentral'nyi Statisticheskii Komitet. 1872. *Sanktpeterburg po Perepis Dekabr 1869 Goda* [St. Petersburg (City) census, December 1869]. St. Petersburg: St. Petersburg Tipografia.

———. 1899-1904. *Pervaia Vseobshchaia Perepis Naseleniia Rossiskoi Imperii 1897 Goda* [First complete census of the empire, 1897 (province volumes)], 89 vols. St. Petersburg: Tipo-lit.

———. 1901. *Raspredlenie Naseleniia po Glavnym Vroispovdaniiam po Dannykh Pervoi Vseobshchei Perepisi 1897*. [Distribution of the population by major religion from the data of the first complete census, 1897]. St. Petersburg: Tipo-lit.

———. 1905a. *Obschi Svod po Imperii Rezulta'tov Razvabotki Dannykh Pervoi Vseobshchei Perepisi Naseleniia, Proizvedennoi 28 Yanvaria 1897 Goda* [Summary volume of the results of the first compete census of the empire, taken on 28 January 1897]. St. Petersburg: Tipo-lit.

———. 1905b. *Raspredlenie Rabochix i Prislygi po Gryppam Zanyiti i po Mesty Rozdeniia na Osnovanyi Dannykh Pervoi Vseobshei Perepisi Naseleniia Rossiskoi*

Imperii 28 Yanvaria 1897 Goda [Distribution of workers and servants by industrial category and by place of birth from data of the first complete census of the empire taken 28 January 1897]. St. Petersburg: Tipo-lit.

―――. 1915. *Ezhegodnik Rossii 1914* [Yearbook of Russia 1914]. St. Petersburg.

Sabagh, G. 1973. Migration and Fertility in Morocco. Paper presented at the annual meeting of the Population Association of America in New Orleans, April 27-30.

Sanders, J. 1969. The Depressed Area and Labor Mobility: The Eastern Kentucky Case. *Journal of Human Resources* 4(4):437-450.

Simmel, G. 1960. The Metropolis and Metropolitan Life. In *Images of Man*, ed. C. W. Mills. New York: George Braziller and Company.

Simmons, A., Diaz-Briquets, S., and Laquian, A. 1977. *Social Change and Internal Migration*. Ottawa: International Development Research Centre.

Sinha, J. 1957. Differential Fertility and Family Limitation in an Urban Community of Uttar Pradesh. *Population Studies* 11(2):157-169.

Sklyrov, L. F. 1962. *Pereselenie i Zemlestroistvo v Sibiri v Godi Stolypinskoi Agrarnoi Reformi* [Migration and agrarian structure in Siberia in the years of the Stolypin agrarian reforms]. Leningrad: Izdatelstvo Leningradskogo Universiteta.

Speare, A. 1974. Urbanization and Migration in Taiwan. *Economic Development and Cultural Change* 22(2):302-319.

Stouffer, S. A. 1940. Intervening Opportunities: A Theory Relating Mobility and Distance. *American Sociological Review* 5(6):845-867.

Stycos, J. M. 1968. *Human Fertility in Latin America*. Ithaca: Cornell University Press.

de Tegoborskii, M. L. 1972. *Commentaries on the Productive Forces of Russia*, 2 volumes. New York: Johnson Reprint Company (reprint of publication of Longman, Brown, Green and Longmans, London 1855).

Todaro, M. P. 1969. A Model of Labor Migration and Unemployment in Less Developed Countries. *American Economic Review* 59:138-148.

Treadgold, D. W. 1957. *The Great Siberian Migration*. Princeton: Princeton University Press.

Tsuru, S. 1963. The Take-off in Japan (1868-1900). In *The Economics of Take-off Into Sustained Growth*, ed. W. W. Rostow. New York: St. Martin's Press.

Tugan-Baranovskii, M. 1898. *Russkaia Fabrika*. 2nd ed. St. Petersburg: L. F. Panteleva.

Volin, L. 1970. *A Century of Russian Agriculture*. Cambridge: Harvard University Press.

Von Laue, T. 1961. Russian Peasants in the Factory. *Journal of Economic History* 21(1):61-80.

Vucinich, W., ed. 1968. *The Peasant in Nineteenth-Century Russia*. Stanford: Stanford University Press.

Wrigley, E. 1969. *Population and History*. New York: World University Library.

Yatsunsky, V. 1974. The Industrial Revolution in Russia. In *Russian Economic Development from Peter the Great to Stalin*, ed. W. L. Blackwell. New York: New Viewpoints.

INDEX

Library of Congress Cataloging in Publication Data

Anderson, Barbara A
    Internal migration during modernization in late
nineteenth-century Russia.

    Revision of the author's thesis, Princeton University,
1974.
    Bibliography: p.
    Includes index.
    1.   Migration, Internal—Russia—History—19th cen-
tury.   2.   Russia—Population—History—19th century.
I.   Title.
HB2067.A52   1980   304.8'2'0947   80-7509
ISBN 0-691-09386-5